# YOU CAN SAVE A BUNDLE ON YOUR CAR INSURANCE

# You Can Save a Bundle on Your Car Insurance

by **Paul Majka**

St. Martin's Press, New York

This book is dedicated to you,
the neglected auto policyholder,
who up to now never had a chance
to fight back.

---

 For information, write: St. Martin's Press, 175 Fifth Avenue, New York, N.Y. 10010
Manufactured in the United States of America

Library of Congress Cataloging in Publication Data

Majka, Paul.
You can save a bundle on your car insurance.

1. Insurance, Automobile—Handbooks, manuals, etc.
I. Title.
HG9970.M34 368.5'72'00202 81-21507
AACR2
ISBN 0-312-89679-4 (pbk.)

Design by Mina Greenstein

10 9 8 7 6 5 4 3 2 1

First Edition

# Contents

*Author's Note* *ix*
*Introduction* *xi*

**1. Understanding Your Rate Classification—You Can Lower Your Rates and Have Your Premium Overpayments Refunded** **1**

The Multi-Car Discount/Vehicle Add-on Discount *5*

Age, Sex, and Marital Status *7*

Operator License Experience *13*

Your Accident and Violation Record —The D.M.V. Report *23*

Vehicle Use *25*

Annual Mileage *32*

Where the Vehicle Is Garaged *38*

Number of Vehicles *40*

Collision and Comprehensive Coverages *41*

Limits of Liability, Uninsured Motorist Coverage, No-Fault and Medical Payments Coverages *47*

**2. The Youthful Driver—How to Get the Affordable Rate** **56**

The Nonprincipal Operator Classification *56*

The Multi-Car, Driver Training, and Good Student Discounts *57*

Other Valuable Saving Tips *66*

**3. Learning the Rules—The Art of Keeping a Low Rate** **71**

The Benefits of Maintaining a Clean Driving Record *71*

How to Avoid and Successfully Contest the Speeding Ticket *71*

How to Prove Your Innocence in Traffic Accidents *73*

How to Avoid Premium Surcharges and Rate Hike Penalties *79*

**4. How to Recognize a Good Car Insurance Deal** **82**

How to Avoid Car Insurance Rip-offs and Exorbitant Rates *83*

How to Choose the Best Insurance Representative *89*

**5. Shopping Around—On the Road to Lower Rates** **91**

The Art of Finding the Rock-Bottom Rates *91*

How to Switch Insurance Companies for Maximum Premium Savings *95*

Finding a Lower Rate with a Poor Driving Record *100*

**6. A Final Word** **102**

Getting Help from Your State Insurance Department *102*

*State Insurance Departments* *104*

*Index* *110*

# Author's Note

This book was written to make the subject of car insurance more comprehensible to the average auto insurance policyholder. Because of the complex nature of the material, I have had to generalize and simplify many of the more complicated issues, and some of the legal questions, that confront every driver. Do not rely entirely on the information presented here. Rather, consult with your own insurance representative, your insurance company, or, if you feel it necessary, your state insurance department before making any changes.

The opinions expressed in this book are solely the author's, and are not intended to be dispositive with regard to any specific issues or questions. The ideas and information contained in this volume are intended merely to be advisory and are to be used at the discretion of the reader.

# Introduction

I don't know how to break this to you, but most drivers are paying too much for their car insurance!

For instance, have you ever wondered why your premiums haven't gone down even though you have been driving carefully for years? Or why, all of a sudden, your premium took a big jump? These situations are caused by a misclassification by the insurance representatives, by the drivers' lack of knowledge, or by the insurance companies' rate hikes.

Most drivers submit themselves to higher than necessary rates by being totally unaware of the factors that entitle them to considerable discounts and other sizable premium credits. For example, a simple change of jobs, a rearrangement of transportation methods, or a leave of absence from work can entitle you to a rate reduction of up to 25 percent. Also, youthful drivers or their parents can cut their premiums by 35–48 percent with a few simple changes. And simply knowing how to shop around can save you 50 percent or better each and every year!

I discovered these shocking conditions during my first years as an insurance agent and since then have devoted myself exclusively to helping the forgotten and bewildered car insurance policyholder. For instance, one case I handled concerning a twenty-two-year-old mother who was paying $600 a year by being classified as under twenty-five and unmarried. I was able to insure her for $300.

I had another case in which a twenty-six-year-old married man was being billed for $850 a year simply because he had received one minor moving violation during his entire driving lifetime. After reviewing his situation, I was able to reduce his premium to $350—a savings of $500 a year!

Then there was the case of a senior citizen who had a perfect driving record but was told by his representative that his auto insurance company was no longer doing business in New York. He was informed that he had to be placed in the assigned risk pool, which more than doubled his premium. I was able to rescue the poor man from this fraudulent scheme and he regained his original rate.

Even if one is fortunate enough not to be victimized as in the preceding cases, at any given time, and in any given geographic area, even under identical circumstances and with identical coverages, the car insurance rates among insurance companies can vary tremendously. For example, if you shop around for auto quotes from companies A, B, C, and D, you'll be shocked to discover that although company A's rate is $600 a year, company B's $450 and company C's $550, while company D has the lowest rate with only a $400-a-year premium.

As you can plainly see, the savings derived from shopping around can amount to thousands of dollars over the years. It is worth the effort to become more knowledgeable on this subject. I wrote this book to share this knowledge with you, and help you acquire the expertise to enjoy the very lowest auto insurance rates year after year.

# 1

# Understanding Your Rate Classification—You Can Lower Your Rates and Have Your Premium Overpayments Refunded

The following factors determine your rate classification. Each can be either modified or circumvented to produce a lower car insurance bill. The suggested maneuvers are perfectly legal and require only simple modifications of one's driving habits or circumstances to bring about remarkable savings. The most used rate classification factors are:

- Age, sex, marital status, and premium discounts
- Operator license experience
- Your accident and violation record—D.M.V. report
- Vehicle use

- Annual mileage
- Where the vehicle is garaged
- Number of vehicles
- Collision and comprehensive coverages
- Limits of liability, uninsured motorist coverage, no-fault and medical payments coverages

Every time you are rated by an insurance company or its representative, these factors are weighed to establish your particular rate classification, which in turn determines your final premium bill. On the surface, this may seem like a very complicated process, but once you understand it you will be able to ask your representative, who is either an insurance agent or an independent insurance broker, the appropriate questions that are instrumental in lowering your overall insurance premium.

The main difference between an insurance *agent* and a *broker* is that an agent works exclusively for one insurance company while a broker works for himself, subcontracting with various insurance companies. Therefore, the honesty, integrity, personal service, and price competitiveness of both should be your primary concern when selecting your personal insurance representative. Both are licensed by the same state insurance department, allowing them to earn commissions ranging from 10 percent to 20 percent of your annual premium. Since you can't get a telephone quote or the car insurance without their involvement, it is important you realize that the easiest way to get the best rate and representative is through knowing the auto insurance principles and cost-saving techniques that are outlined in this book.

The sooner you learn the rate classification factors and the cost-saving techniques, the sooner you will start saving yourself a bundle each and every year.

Let's start off with a typical insurance bill for an adult with a clean driving record who owns a five-year-old medium-priced car and lives in a mid-sized city of 30,000. I will refer to this standard example throughout the book to point out the savings you can obtain by making various changes in your rate classification and coverage.

| | |
|---|---|
| Bodily injury liability<br>$10,000 per person; $20,000 each occurrence | $40 |
| Property Damage Liability<br>$5,000 each occurrence | $30 |
| Medical payments (if carried) | |

| Coverage | Premium |
|---|---|
| No-fault personal injury protection (where mandatory) | $28 |
| Uninsured motorist—bodily injury $10,000 each person; $20,000 each occurrence | $2 |
| Automobile collision—actual cash value Less deductible of $100 | $60 |
| Automobile comprehensive—actual cash value less deductible of $50 with full glass coverage | $20 |
| Semiannual premium | $180 |
| Annual premium | $360 |

If the same person lived in a rural town with a small population and therefore a scarcity of cars and accidents, his premium would be considerably less and would probably range between $280 and $320 a year. However, if he lived in a large metropolitan area, the premium could run as high as $500 to $800 or more a year. As you can see, insurance bills can vary more than $500 on the basis of geographic location alone.

All insurance companies give the 1.00 rate factor to adult/married drivers: married females at any age; married males ages 25 and older; single females ages 25 and older; and single males ages 30 and older.

The annual premiums will differ among

these adult/married groups because of the huge differences in the insurance companies' base premium rates. For example, an adult/married male will receive a 1.00 rate factor from either company A, B, or C. However, the base premium rates for these companies will vary tremendously, now as well as in the future, causing the divergence in their final premium amounts. The base premium rates for, let's say, bodily injury liability limits of 25/50 could be $40 for company A ($40 × 1.00 = $40), $50 for company B ($50 × 1.00 = $50), and maybe $55 for company C ($55 × 1.00 = $55), while a year from now, the premium schedule could be completely reversed!

In this example, our adult male received a 1.00 rate factor from all three companies; however, he would have saved $15 a year or 37½ percent annually by shopping around for company A's current rate—that's why it's so important to know the art of shopping around.

## The Multi-Car Discount/Vehicle Add-on Discount

One of the most overlooked areas of car insurance savings yet one of its most productive is the multi-car/vehicle add-on discount. Most drivers who qualify achieve annual savings of up to 20 percent. However, there are millions of drivers who are still unaware of this discount's existence and, therefore, are missing out on its premium savings benefits.

Simply stated, the multi-car/vehicle add-on discount is given to those drivers who insure all of their vehicles (two or more) with one insurance company. Those who insure their cars, vans, pickup trucks, mobile homes, snowmobiles, trailers, and campers with the same company enjoy a discount of approximately 20 percent compared to those who insure their vehicles separately. The only exception to this rule is that motorcycles, mopeds, dune buggies, and motor scooters are not classified as private passenger vehicles but rather as separate entities and must be insured with their own individual policies without receiving the benefit of the 20 percent discount.

The following examples will help to clarify the multi-car/vehicle add-on's economizing effect while also explaining how it can be used to your best advantage: A newlywed or married couple (ages 25 and older) could reduce their total annual insurance bill by 20 percent simply by insuring both cars with one of their insurance companies. Instead of insuring separately, and paying a $720 undiscounted premium ($360 individual auto rate × 2 cars = $720), they could insure both cars with one company and reduce their total bill to only $576, saving $144 annually ($360 individual auto rate × 2 cars = $720 × .80 multi-car/vehicle add-on discount = $576).

The same result could be achieved if this couple started out with only one car but later added a nonreplacement (additional) car, pickup truck, van, mobile home, camper, or trailer ($360 individual auto rate × 2 vehicles = $720 × .80 multi-car/vehicle add-on discount = $576).

It definitely works in your favor to insure all of your vehicles with the same insurance company. However, as an added bonus, this astute practice makes it easier for you to take advantage of the many other premium-reducing strategies and techniques that are explained in the ensuing sections and chapters. *Never insure separately when you can discount your premiums with one easy step.*

## Age, Sex, and Marital Status

Because statistics prove that as separate groups young single males and single females have more accidents and moving violations than their older and married counterparts, their premium rating factors are much higher than the national average of 1.00. However, if you fall into either of these categories, do not despair. There are several premium saving options available to you. Before we delve into these premium saving maneuvers, you should know the exact age, sex, and marital status breakdowns standard among most insurance companies throughout the country. The highest-rated group is that of single males under age 21, followed by ages 21–24 and then 25–29, with the rates decreasing at each higher age bracket. The following rating factors pertain to principal operators—those who drive at least 25 percent of the total mileage and have their vehicles registered in their own names.

Single males under age 21 have a rating factor that can vary from 2.00 to 3.00 depending on the company—double to triple the normal premium charged to an adult male (30 and older) or a married male 25 or older. Compared to our standard example, in which the adult/married premium is $360 (based on a 1.00 rating factor), the final premium for a single male under 21 would range from a low of $720 ($360 × 2.00) to a high of $1,080 ($360 × 3.00), depending upon the rating factor used by the insurance company. As you can see, the premium differences among various companies can be quite staggering. In this case, you could save as much as 33 percent every year by simply knowing how to shop around, a subject we'll be examining in depth in Chapter 5, Shopping Around—On the Road to Lower Rates.

Single males aged 21–24 have a rating factor that can vary from 1.75 to 2.50. This means that their final premiums can range from a low of \$630 (\$360 × 1.75) to as much as \$900 (\$360 × 2.50). Again, the differences in the premiums are staggering, and in this case a single male could save 30 percent just by shopping for the insurance company with the lower \$630 rate.

Single males aged 25–29, who have a rating factor from 1.25 to 1.75, may have premiums ranging from a low of \$450 (\$360 × 1.25) to a high of \$630 (\$360 × 1.75). The staggering 29 percent contrast between these two premiums is due entirely to the arbitrary use of different rating factors among the various insurance companies.

Young married males are given a better rating break than their single counterparts, and for those who are newlywed and under age 21, rating factors can vary from a low of 1.40 to a high of 2.00. Their final premiums will thus range between $504 ($360 × 1.40) and $720.00 ($360 × 2.00). It certainly pays to shop around for the 30 percent or greater savings that many lower-cost insurance companies offer.

Married males between the ages of 21 and 24 can have a rating factor that varies between 1.00 and 1.40, which means that their final premiums can range from $360 ($360 × 1.00) to $504 ($360 × 1.40) for a difference of 29 percent.

Married males aged 25 and older and single males aged 30 and older are both given the low adult/married rate of 1.00, as in our standard example, which results in a $360 premium ($360 × 1.00).

There are numerous premium-slashing adjustments and maneuvers available to all drivers regardless of age, sex, or marital status that will be explored in depth in the upcoming rate classification sections. But first, let's examine the various female age and marital status classifications.

Single females are treated more generously than their single male counterparts simply because of their more favorable driving statistics. On the average, single females pay 25 percent to 35 percent less than single males in each of the age categories. They are even given the adult/married rate classification at the age of 25 whether they are married or not. However, even though single females receive a better premium break than single males, the female rating factors can vary considerably from one company to another. This permits even more savings for those who take the time to shop around. For example, the under age 21 group's rating factor can vary from a low of 1.75 to a high of 2.25, which means that their final premiums can range from $630 ($360 × 1.75) to as much as $810 ($360 × 2.25) for a 22 percent annual difference.

Single females aged 21–24 have a rating factor that may vary from 1.40 to 1.75. Their final premiums range anywhere from $504 ($360 × 1.40) to $630 ($360 × 1.75)—a 20 percent difference.

Once a woman marries or turns 25, she immediately qualifies for the 1.00 adult/married rate factor, even though married males have to wait until age 25 to receive it and single males must wait until age 30.

It is interesting to note that certain insurance companies give an additional discount of 10 percent to single females aged 30–64 who are the only licensed drivers in their households. In those cases, the rating factor is lowered to a .90, which, modifying our standard example, would produce a final premium of $324 ($360 × .90). Again, it's advantageous to shop around. (See Chapter 5.)

The final age classification is for senior citizens of either sex who are age 65 and older. They are eligible for a discount of about 10 percent, which produces a rating factor of .90 and a final premium of $324.

Newlywed males under age 30 and newly married females under age 25 should notify their insurance representatives of their marriage promptly if they don't want to risk the chance of not receiving the adult/married rate on their next renewal period. Insurance representatives must be updated on the vital changes that affect your overall insurance rates. If you neglect to inform them of these significant changes, chances are that you'll deprive yourself of many sizable premium discounts and credits, such as the adult/married discount, the multi-car discount (insuring two or more vehicles on the same policy), the low mileage discount (driving less than 7,500 miles annually), and the limited usage discounts (driving for pleasure and limited driving to work). The combined cost-reducing effects of these discounts can save you well over 50 percent on your premium each and every year.

Females under age 25 or males under age 30 can easily lose the adult/married discount if they are divorced. If you have been divorced recently and fall into these age and sex categories, your new single status could be brought to your insurance company's attention through your own representative if you change cars or your address. If you apply for a policy with a new company, your new single status would become evident. However, if there are children involved in the divorce, the party who is given their permanent custody may be able to retain the married rate while the other party is considered single again and rated accordingly. But keep in mind that although all insurance companies treat divorce in the same manner, they do not all give married status to the party who retains the children. Therefore, if your insurance company isn't lenient in this regard, I advise you to shop around for a more liberal company in order to save your rate classification plus a lot of premium dollars.

## Operator License Experience

Most insurance companies prefer to insure experienced drivers who have three or more years of license experience over inexperienced drivers with less than three years' experience. Inexperienced drivers attempting to get an auto policy in their own names are rated as if they are likely to be involved in an accident in the near future.

Most inexperienced drivers are placed in their state's Assigned Risk Plan, also known in some states as the Automobile Insurance Plan, Reinsurance Facilities, State Funds, Joint Underwriting Associations, or simply the Risk Pool. Basically, the Assigned Risk Plan was designed to insure inexperienced drivers as well as drivers with poor driving records who are considered too substandard to be insured in the regular market at standard rates. Since these drivers have to be insured in some way, individual states have designed their own risk pools, which are quite similar to each other, but are called by various names.

The first rule an inexperienced driver should remember is to avoid getting an individual policy. You will wind up in your state's Assigned Risk Plan, paying its exorbitant rates. New drivers should make every effort to be added to either their spouse's or parent's policy as an additional or occasional driver. You'll be charged the standard rates and save yourself a lot of premium dollars and aggravation.

For example, if you're a single person living

at home, you could have yourself classified as a nonprincipal and occasional driver and thereby cut your premium bill in half—see Chapter 2.

**Single Males**

| *Individual Policy* | | *vs.* | *Nonprincipal Operator Add-on* | *Savings* | *%* |
|---|---|---|---|---|---|
| less than 21 | $720 | | $374 | $346 | 48% |
| 21–24 | $630 | | $328 | $302 | 48% |

**Single Females**

| *Individual Policy* | | *vs.* | *Nonprincipal Operator Add-on* | *Savings* | *%* |
|---|---|---|---|---|---|
| less than 21 | $630 | | $328 | $302 | 48% |
| 21–24 | $504 | | $262 | $242 | 48% |

If you're a married person as well as a new driver, you could save the following amounts by being added on to your spouse's policy:

**Married Males**

| *Individual Policy* | | *vs.* | *Add-on to Wife's Policy* | *Savings* | *%* |
|---|---|---|---|---|---|
| less than 21 | $600 | | $403 | $197 | 33% |
| 21–24 | $500 | | $350 | $150 | 30% |
| 25+ | $400 | | $288 | $112 | 28% |

**Married Females**

| | *Individual Policy* | *vs.* | *Add-on to Husband's Policy* | *Savings* | *%* |
|---|---|---|---|---|---|
| any age | $500 | | $288 | $212 | 42% |

Remember that as an add-on to either your parent's or spouse's policy, your driving mistakes affect not only your own record and rates, but theirs as well. Since a moving violation can increase the overall premium by 10 percent and an at-fault accident can do the same damage by 20–40 percent, your cautious driving will not only pay off in lower rates, but also in better family relationships.

For those inexperienced drivers who have no other choice but to take out an individual policy and pay the assigned risk rates, I suggest that you free yourself and your car from any bank lien so that you won't be burdened with the extra comprehensive and collision coverages. You would save the following amounts:

**Single Males**

| | *Individual Policy with Comp. & Collision* | *vs.* | *Premium without Comp. & Collision* | *Savings* | *%* |
|---|---|---|---|---|---|
| less than 21 | $720 | | $400 | $320 | 44% |
| 21–24 | $630 | | $350 | $280 | 44% |
| 25–29 | $500 | | $300 | $200 | 40% |

**Single Females**

| | *Individual Policy with Comp. & Collision* | *vs.* | *Premium without Comp. & Collision* | *Savings* | *%* |
|---|---|---|---|---|---|
| less than 21 | $630 | | $350 | $280 | 44% |
| 21–24 | $504 | | $280 | $224 | 44% |

**Married Males**

| | *Individual Policy with Comp. & Collision* | *vs.* | *Premium without Comp. & Collision* | *Savings* | *%* |
|---|---|---|---|---|---|
| less than 21 | $600 | | $376 | $224 | 37% |
| 21–24 | $500 | | $340 | $160 | 32% |
| 25 + | $400 | | $280 | $120 | 30% |

**Married Females**

| | *Individual Policy with Comp. & Collision* | *vs.* | *Premium without Comp. & Collision* | *Savings* | *%* |
|---|---|---|---|---|---|
| any age | $500 | | $300 | $200 | 40% |

As mentioned previously, inexperienced operators should drive with extra caution since they can hardly afford to pay the additional 10 percent penalty per moving violation nor the 20–40 percent surcharge per at-fault accident on top of their already inflated rates. For example, a series of moving violations and at-fault accidents would drastically affect the rates of inexperienced single drivers in the following way:

**Single Males**

| Individual Policy with Comp. & Collision | | | Moving Violation at 10% | | At-Fault Accident at 20% | | New Surcharged Prem. | % |
|---|---|---|---|---|---|---|---|---|
| less than 21 | $720 | + | $72 | + | $144 | = | $936 | 30% |
| 21–24 | $630 | + | $63 | + | $126 | = | $819 | 30% |

**Single Females**

| Individual Policy with Comp. & Collision | | | Moving Violation at 10% | | At-Fault Accident at 20% | | New Surcharged Prem. | % |
|---|---|---|---|---|---|---|---|---|
| less than 21 | $630 | + | $63 | + | $126 | = | $819 | 30% |
| 21–24 | $504 | + | $50 | + | $101 | = | $655 | 30% |

Obviously, experienced drivers don't have the same premium problems as inexperienced drivers, but all careless and thoughtless drivers pay the same penalty of a 10 percent increment per moving violation and a 20–40 percent surcharge per at-fault accident. Therefore, it pays for all of us to drive cautiously in order to maintain our clean or nearly clean driving records.

Divorcees may be entitled to the same kind of premium refund as parents. If your ex-husband or ex-wife had a poor driving record and you have continued to pay their old surcharged rates since they left your household permanently, bring this to the immediate attention of your insurance representative. Visit him with all pertinent and documented information so that your premiums can be reduced immediately while your application for a premium refund is processed.

For example, if you were separated or divorced a year ago but forgot that you were still paying a $600 premium based on a two-car family, you would be eligible for an immediate rate reduction to $360 (based on only your car) and a premium refund of $240. If you had neglected to inform your insurance company for two years, you would be entitled to a $480 refund, and so on.

If your insurance company procrastinates or refuses outright to pay the refund, your state insurance department (Consumer Affairs Division) will help you with a legitimate complaint. As a last resort, you have the option of taking the matter to a small-claims court or to your attorney. See sample letters A and B.

## SAMPLE LETTER A

Requesting the reduction of your auto insurance premium and the remittance of your refund check.

9/20/81

John/Jane Policyholder
110 Washington Ave.
Anywhere, U.S.A.
Policy # 60-475-120-89

A.B.C. Insurance Company
250 State St.
Anywhere, U.S.A.

Dear A.B.C. Insurance Company:

Two years ago, my husband and I were legally separated; we were divorced last year.

During this entire two-year period, my husband lived in his own apartment. However, I understand that your records show that we're still married and living together, which is in error.

After discussing this with my agent/broker, I realized that my insurance rate during the last two years didn't reflect my husband's departure and that my premium should have been substantially reduced at that time.

Therefore, my agent/broker requested that my premium be reduced from $600 a year to $360 and I be sent a refund check for $480 as reimbursement for the last two years of overpayments.

In cooperation with my agent/broker, I've enclosed photocopies of my legal separation, divorce decree, and my ex-husband's rent receipts to assist you with the prompt reduction of my premium and to support the timely remittance of my refund check.

Thank you for your immediate attention and full cooperation in this matter.

Sincerely,
John/Jane Policyholder

## SAMPLE LETTER B

Requesting your state insurance department to assist you with the refund check.

10/21/81

John/Jane Policyholder
110 Washington Ave.
Anywhere, U.S.A.
Policy # 60-475-120-89

State Insurance Department
Division of Consumer Affairs
100 Capitol St.
Anystate, U.S.A.

Dear Insurance Department:

I enclose a copy of my letter dated 9/20/81, which I sent to the A.B.C. Insurance Company requesting the reduction of my auto insurance premium and the timely remittance of my refund check. I also enclosed copies of my legal separation, my divorce decree, and my ex-husband's rent receipts for the past two years.

Although the A.B.C. Insurance Company reduced my premium from $600 a year to $360, I still haven't received my $480 refund check. Therefore, I request your immediate assistance in lieu of my taking this to a small-claims court, or my giving this to my attorney for additional action, or my taking this up with my congressman.

Please contact me as soon as possible so that this urgent matter can be settled promptly.

Again, thank you for your timely assistance.

Sincerely,
John/Jane Policyholder

cc: A.B.C. Insurance Company

## Your Accident and Violation Record—The D.M.V. Report

My adage, that a clean record today keeps the high rates away, is truer now than ever. Since the advent of the computer age, all moving violations and reported accidents show up on your Department of Motor Vehicles (D.M.V.) Report even if they occurred out of state, while driving a borrowed or rented car, or while driving a company vehicle on the job.

The insurance companies hold these transgressions against our records for anywhere from three to five years, depending upon state law and individual company policy. Two or more transgressions or a combination of two or more moving violations and reported at-fault accidents may not only substantially raise your rates, but will also force you to stay with the same company, paying its high premiums, in the hope of not getting canceled and thrown into the assigned risk pool, where it could be even worse!

For example, suppose you're a New York State driver who received a speeding ticket during a winter vacation in Florida and that you then slid on the ice on the way home, causing $1,000 damage to your car, which you reported to your insurance company. After paying the claim, less a $100 deductible, your insurance company suddenly raises your rates by 50 percent—from $360 to $540 (10 percent for the speeding ticket and another 40 percent for the accident). After getting over the initial shock, you make a few phone calls and discover that there are several more liberal companies that wouldn't have raised your rates for either the speeding ticket or the accident since the damage was caused only to your car rather than to someone else's property. However, because of a statewide underwriting rule that prevents companies from accepting risks with two or more incidents within a three-year period, these other companies must refuse to write you a policy. Upon further investigation, you discover that if you left your present company now, you would wind up in the assigned risk pool, where your rate would be $600—$60 more than what you're paying now.

In effect, you would be stuck with the same company for the next three years while paying them an extra $540 in premiums ($540.00 − $360.00 = $180 × 3 years = $540). This is the kind of havoc that moving violations and accidents can cause to your overall premium by preventing you from shopping around while forcing you to pay exorbitant rates to the very company that's punishing you.

Since your driving record is so critical to your pursuit of lower car insurance premiums, if you're not sure about your driving history over the past three years, you should order a copy of your driving record either from your State Department of Motor Vehicles or from the State Police. The small fee that they charge is well worth paying because the information can be used later to save you money as well as needless grief.

If you have had a good driving record over the past three years, you're already on the right track. If your record is poor, don't give up. You can always straighten out your record in the future—and use this book to save you money during the waiting period. (See Chapter 5, items 9 and 10.)

## Vehicle Use

Car insurance rates vary from person to person according to how they use their vehicles. The lowest usage category is for full-time farming. The next lowest category is for pleasure use, which includes driving to work less than 30 miles roundtrip per week. The next categories are for vehicle use for work between 30 and 100 miles per week and for work over 100 miles per week. The highest category is for business use such as on-the-road sales, light delivery work, and other jobs requiring the continuous commercial use of a vehicle.

Each usage category has its own rating factor, which is determined by the amount of risk associated with that driving pattern. The following examples will help you understand how these various categories affect our rates:

| *Usage* | *Rate Factor* | × | *Base Premium* | = | *Final Premium* |
|---|---|---|---|---|---|
| Farm use | .80 | × | $360 | = | $288 |
| Pleasure use including driving to work less than 30 roundtrip miles per week | 1.00 | × | $360 | = | $360 |
| Driving to work 30–100 roundtrip miles per week | 1.10 | × | $360 | = | $396 |
| Driving to work over 100 round-trip miles per week | 1.20 | × | $360 | = | $432 |
| Business use | 1.30 | × | $360 | = | $468 |

Your usage category is determined at the time you apply for the insurance or when you notify your representative of any changes in your driving pattern. Therefore, your insurance company classifies you according to the information you give to its agents or brokers. Remember, though, that the company has the option to make an occasional spot check or a phone call to verify its records.

Not everyone can be a full-time farmer or use a car exclusively for pleasure. But by making a few simple changes in your driving habits, you can place yourself in a lower usage category and save a lot of premium dollars.

For instance, if you're married and have two cars in the family, arrange to have the older car driven to work while leaving the newer one at home to be rated for pleasure use. This maneuver can save you as much as 20 percent if comprehensive and collision coverages are carried on the newer vehicle. If the annual premium for the comprehensive and collision coverages is $192 and you drive more than 100 miles roundtrip to work each week ($160 [base premium] × 1.20 [greater than 100 miles to work rate factor] = $192), you could save $32 a year simply by switching cars and driving the older car to work ($160 [base premium] × 1.00 [pleasure use rate factor] = $160). You could save even more simply by car pooling or by taking public transportation to work, since you would then lower your usage category for all your cars and insurance coverages. For example, instead of paying $432 a year for all of that extra driving ($360 × 1.20 [greater than 100 miles to work rate factor] = $432), you could be paying only $360 based on the 1.00 pleasure usage (or less than 30 roundtrip miles to work rate factor) and thereby save a hefty $72 a year (20 percent) plus a lot of gasoline and wear and tear on your car.

As you can see, any reduction in work-driving miles within the preceding guidelines or the elimination of any business-use driving can save you from 10 to 30 percent. Notify your insurance representative whenever you make a permanent change. If you forget and so inform him at a later date, you still will be entitled to an immediate rate reduction *plus* a premium refund for the time you were incorrectly billed. For example, say you started taking the bus to work three years ago rather than driving over 100 roundtrip miles every week and forgot to notify your insurance representative. Once you informed him of the change, you would be entitled to an immediate rate reduction from $432 to $360 *plus* a premium refund of $216 ($72 × 3 years). Of course, you would be required to provide sufficient proof to substantiate the change, such as bus ticket stubs or checks for commuter tickets, but it certainly would be worth the effort.

It is also a good idea to call your representative to make sure that your current driving usage pattern is classified properly by the insurance company. If it isn't, you will be eligible for a rate reduction plus a refund for any past overcharges. You can check this simply by asking your representative how you are rated for vehicle use and then comparing the answer to your actual driving pattern.

If you have been adversely misclassified, make that fact known and request a new classification with its corresponding lower rates as well as a premium refund if applicable. See sample letters C and D.

## SAMPLE LETTER C

Requesting the reduction of your auto insurance premium and the remittance of your refund check.

9/20/81

John/Jane Policyholder
110 Washington Ave.
Anywhere, U.S.A.
Policy # 60-475-120-89

A.B.C. Insurance Company
250 State St.
Anywhere, U.S.A.

Dear A.B.C. Insurance Company:

Because I changed jobs three years ago and work closer to my home, I've been taking the bus to work every morning instead of driving my car.

After discussing this with my agent/broker, I realize that my premium had not taken this into account and that I've been charged a rate that was based on my driving over 100 miles to work every week which, of course, is in error.

Therefore, my agent/broker requested that my premium be reduced from $432 a year to $360 and that I be sent a refund check for $216 as reimbursement for my three years of overpayments.

In cooperation with my agent/broker, I've enclosed photocopies of my current work record, pay stubs, and bus ticket receipts for the past three years to assist you with the prompt reduction of my premium and to support the timely remittance of my refund check.

I thank you for your immediate attention and full cooperation in this matter.

Sincerely,
John/Jane policyholder

## SAMPLE LETTER D

Requesting your state insurance department to assist you with the refund check.

10/21/81

John/Jane Policyholder
110 Washington Ave.
Anywhere, U.S.A.
Policy # 60-475-120-89

State Insurance Department
Division of Consumer Affairs
100 Capitol St.
Anystate, U.S.A.

Dear Insurance Department:

I enclose a copy of my letter dated 9/20/81 that I sent to the A.B.C. Insurance Company requesting the reduction of my auto insurance premium and the timely remittance of my refund check. I also enclose copies of my current work records, pay stubs, and bus ticket receipts that I referred to in my letter.

Although the A.B.C. Insurance Company reduced my premium from $432 to $360 a year, I still haven't received my $216 refund check. Therefore, I request your immediate assistance in lieu of my taking this to a small-claims court, or my giving this to my attorney for additional action, or my taking this up with my congressman.

Please contact me as soon as possible so that this urgent matter can be settled promptly.

Again, I thank you for your timely assistance.

Sincerely,
John/Jane Policyholder

cc: A.B.C. Insurance Company

## Annual Mileage

Most vehicles are rated according to how many miles they are driven and are placed in either the high mileage (over 7,500 miles annually) or low mileage (less than 7,500 miles annually) category. This rating decision is made at the time you take out the insurance or when you change or add cars to your existing policy. The underwriting decision placing you in either the high or low mileage category is based on your past driving history or on your present odometer reading. Many insurance companies require odometer proof before giving the 15 percent low mileage discount which, in our example, is quite substantial ($360 × .15 = $54 discount).

If you have always been given the low mileage discount in the past, there is a better chance that your insurance company will continue the practice when you purchase replacement (nonadditional) vehicles. However, it wouldn't be a bad idea to call your representative to verify its continuation or to demand its reinstatement if it was inadvertently left off your new policy.

On the other hand, if you purchase an additional new or used car, your company may require odometer proof from your agent or broker verifying that it is being driven less than 7,500 miles a year. For example, if you bought an additional new car, the odometer would have to read less than 3,750 miles in six months or less than 7,500 miles in one year, depending upon your company's policy, to qualify for the low mileage discount. If you purchased an additional used car, your representative would compare the odometer reading at the time of the purchase to the actual reading in six months or a year to prove the lower mileage. If you bought a used car with 50,000 miles on it, the odometer would have to read less than 53,750 in six months or less than 57,500 a year later to qualify for the low mileage discount.

Another important point to remember is that when you change insurance companies, your new representative will want to know when you purchased your car(s) as well as the present and past odometer readings on each vehicle. In this way, you'll be able either to qualify immediately for the low mileage discount or to qualify at a later date by reducing your overall driving mileage.

Another important point to remember is that if you're driving less these days, you can at any time request a reëvaluation of your mileage and receive the 15 percent discount immediately or at a future date. The above procedure would probably be followed and serves as an example of how to qualify for the low mileage discount. Remember that each vehicle is separately rated. In a multi-car family, all cars, only one, or none at all could qualify for the discount. Therefore, in order for you to benefit fully from the discount, I recommend that each car be driven under the 7,500 mileage mark. But if that's not possible, you'll maximize your savings by taking the low mileage discount on the newer car(s), especially if the comprehensive and collision coverages are carried. For example, if the annual premium for the comprehensive and collision coverages is $160, you'll stand to save an additional $24 by qualifying for the discount ($160 × .15 = $24).

Finally, if in the past you did qualify for the

discount but were recently overlooked and not given the 15 percent credit, you would be immediately entitled to a rate reduction plus a premium refund check for the past overcharges. For example, if you decreased your driving mileage substantially over the past three years to less than 7,500 miles per year but failed to notify your insurance representative, you would be entitled to a lower premium rate of $306 ($360 – $54 [15 percent discount] = $306) plus a refund check for $162 ($54 × 3 years). Naturally you'll have to prove that you did drive less than 7,500 miles each year by odometer readings, but that can be easily verified and shouldn't pose any serious problem. See sample letters E and F.

## SAMPLE LETTER E

Requesting the reduction of your auto insurance premium and the remittance of your refund check.

9/20/81

John/Jane Policyholder
110 Washington Ave.
Anywhere, U.S.A.
Policy # 60-475-120-89

A.B.C. Insurance Company
250 State St.
Anywhere, U.S.A.

Dear A.B.C. Insurance Company:

Three years ago, I bought a used car and insured it with your company. Since then, I've driven very little and, in fact, put on only 12,000 miles over that three-year period—45,000 odometer miles when purchased and currently only 57,000 odometer miles.

After discussing this with my agent/broker I realize that my premiums have not taken my low mileage into account and that I've been charged a rate that was based on my driving over 7,500 miles each year, which, of course, was not the case.

Therefore, my agent/broker requested that my premium be reduced from $360 a year to $306 and that I be sent a refund check for $162 as reimbursement for my three years of over-payments.

In cooperation with my agent/broker, I've enclosed photocopies of my original bill of sale, which verifies the initial 45,000 miles, as well as my annual auto inspection papers, that show each year's odometer readings including this year's with 57,000 miles.

I'm sure that the enclosed documentation

will assist you with the prompt reduction of my premium and support the timely remittance of my refund check.

I thank you for your immediate attention and full cooperation in this matter.

Sincerely,
John/Jane Policyholder

**SAMPLE LETTER F**

Requesting your state insurance department to assist you with the refund check.

10/21/81

John/Jane Policyholder
110 Washington Ave.
Anywhere, U.S.A.
Policy # 60-475-120-89

State Insurance Department
Division of Consumer Affairs
100 Capitol St.
Anystate, U.S.A.

Dear Insurance Department:

I enclose a copy of my letter dated 9/20/81, which I sent to the A.B.C. Insurance Company requesting the reduction of my auto insurance premium and the timely remittance of my refund check. I also enclose copies of my past and present auto inspection records plus the original bill of sale on my car.

Although the A.B.C. Insurance Company reduced my premium from $360 a year to $306, I still haven't received my $162 refund check. Therefore, I request your immediate assistance in lieu of my taking this to a small claims court, my giving this to my attorney for additional action, or my taking this up with my congressman.

Please contact me as soon as possible so that this urgent matter can be settled promptly.

Again, I thank you for your timely assistance.

Sincerely,
John/Jane Policyholder

cc: A.B.C. Insurance Company

### Where the Vehicle Is Garaged

Your insurance rate is also determined by where you live and garage your car. Rating territories are comprised of cities, towns, or counties and are rated according to their accident experience, which usually follows the population density of that particular area. Therefore, sparsely populated areas that experience less accidents enjoy lower rates in contrast to more densely populated places. If you live in a small rural village in a sparsely populated county, your insurance rate in our example could be as low as $280 per year, while if you live in a medium-sized town in that same county, your rate would be $360. On the other hand, if you live in a heavily populated area in the next county, your rate could be as much as $800 for the identical coverage.

Since we live in a mobile society, it's wise to investigate the differences in the territorial rate structures before making a final move. The premium difference can be quite substantial, as previously illustrated, and is therefore worthy of scrutiny. For example, I once rated a case in which a foot marker on the other side of the county line enabled me to save my client an additional $100 a year. It was a matter of a few inches, but it located him in a lower populated county and resulted in a much lower premium.

When you're making plans for a move, call your insurance representative and ask him about the economics of the various territorial rate structures. In particular ask him for the rate differences between the various counties and cities in which you're considering renting or buying a house. If the premium difference between living in a city or in the outlying suburbs amounts to $200 a year, this economic factor should be weighed heavily when making your final decision.

## Number of Vehicles

In order to take advantage of the 20 percent multi-car discount that is available in all states, you should have all your private passenger vehicles insured under one policy. Recreational vehicles, campers, and pickup trucks with less than 7,800 pound gross laden weight capacity that are not used exclusively for wholesale, retail, or other commercial uses are all considered private passenger vehicles.

Most commercial vehicles are insured under a separate commercial auto policy in addition to general liability and other business-type coverages. If you're a businessman with commercial vehicles and business property, you could save a lot of premium dollars simply by shopping around for your fire and liability packages as well as for your commercial auto coverages. I have seen cases in which businessmen have saved thousands of dollars a year by shopping around.

The 20 percent multi-car discount applies to *each* vehicle, so don't lose out by insuring any vehicle with a separate company. For example, if you own both a car and a pickup truck and insure them separately, you could be losing as much as $144 per year by not taking advantage of the discount ($360 premium per vehicle × 2 = $720 combined annual premium × 20 percent lost discount = $144 additional premium per year). *Don't insure separately; always add on to your existing policy.*

## Collision and Comprehensive Coverages

Stated simply, collision coverage pays for the replacement or repair of damages to your insured vehicle caused by the upset, overturning, or collision with another physical object or person. The collision coverage can be purchased with a deductible (the portion of the damage that the insured pays), which can range from a low of $50 to a high of $500. Of course, the higher the deductible, the lower the cost of the coverage.

The comprehensive coverage will pay for the replacement or repair of damage to your vehicle caused by theft, larceny, fire, malicious mischief, vandalism, flying missiles, water damage, flood, hail, windstorm, earthquake, explosion, or any accident with birds or animals and covers glass breakage for all of the above. The comprehensive coverage can be purchased with no deductible in the states of Arkansas, Connecticut, Delaware, Kansas, New Hampshire, Oregon, South Dakota, Texas, Virginia, Utah, Washington, and Wisconsin. The comprehensive coverage can be purchased with a $50, $100, $200, or a $500 deductible in the other states. Again, the higher the deductible, the lower the cost.

Most states require financed vehicles to carry both the comprehensive and the collision coverages for the protection of lending institutions. However, New York and most other states allow the deductibles on coverage for financed vehicles to be as much as $500. Verify your state's maximum limit through your insurance representative. In certain cases, you may be able to negotiate a higher deductible with your lending institution if you have a good credit rating. In any case, using higher deductibles is a smart way for *careful drivers* to save many premium dollars.

It's important to be aware of the cases in which you can legally collect from your own policy. When you cause an accident in which you are clearly at fault or when you're not at fault but are unable to prove your innocence at the accident scene because of a lack of witnesses or other crucial evidence, you may collect from your own policy. You also may collect from it if your vehicle is struck by an unknown hit-and-run driver while it is legally parked or is being driven in a legal manner.

In each of the above cases, your deductible would be subtracted from the total claim and you would collect the difference. However, if you were a victim of an accident and were able to prove your innocence, you would collect fully (without a deductible) from the guilty party's policy. The same would hold true if you were subsequently able to identify the hit-and-run driver and establish your innocence.

With this in mind, there are several rules of thumb that can be used to save money on the collision coverage:

**Collision Coverage Table—**

*Deductible and Annual Premium Amounts*

| *Deductible* | | *Annual Premium* |
|---|---|---|
| $100 | = | $160 |
| $200 | = | $120 |
| $250 | = | $ 90 |
| $500 | = | $ 50 |

1. As the above table shows, you could raise your collision deductible to equal your weekly paycheck. If you did so, that amount is all that you would be risking if you had to make a claim against your own policy. For ex-

ample, if you raised the amount of your deductible from \$100 to \$250, you would save \$70 a year (\$160 – \$90 = \$70) which would cover the \$150 difference between the \$250 deductible and the \$100 deductible in a little over two years. Obviously, the more carefully you drive, the more money you can save. In this instance, if you didn't have an accident in ten years, you would save \$700 (\$70.00 savings × 10 years = \$700).

2. In most cases, the older the car, the less sense it makes to carry the collision coverage. This is especially true for cars six or more years old that have diminishing book values. However, in recent years, certain economy and foreign cars not only have kept up but increased their "Blue Book" values. A good rule of thumb to remember is that if a car is worth at least \$1,500, then it makes sense to carry the collision coverage. However, refer to rule 1 for maximum premium savings.

3. If you have always been a careful driver and never had to make a collision claim against your own policy, it could make sense to drop the coverage entirely and save the difference regardless of the age of your car. However, if you make this choice to do so I

advise you not to lend your car to anyone, since you then would be playing Russian roulette with your own policy. Also, be sure that you know how to make a *successful* claim against a careless driver if you're ever involved in an accident in order to have the guilty party's policy pay for your collision damage. The accident and claim rules will be fully explained in Chapter 3.

4. In recent years, more and more insurance companies have been basing their comprehensive and collision rates not so much on the cost of cars, but on the historic loss experience of the various models. Their studies have found that certain models consistently have fewer accident and theft claims and are less expensive to repair than many other models. As a result, many companies have scaled down their comprehensive and collision rates for those particular models which, in many cases, can mean savings of $50 or more a year. When considering buying a new or almost new car, it would be a good idea to call your insurance representative and ask for the comprehensive and collision rates for the various models you've been considering. That way you can make a more intelligent decision.

5. The comprehensive coverage is an entirely different story, since it covers the mischievous deeds of people and the uncontrollable acts of God, which have nothing to do with the manner in which we drive. Therefore, in most cases I recommend the retention of this coverage, coupled with a low deductible because of the reasonableness of the premiums. However, if you wish to lower the premium cost, you can raise the amount of the deductible to suits your needs:

**Comprehensive Coverage Table—**
*Deductible and Annual Premium Amounts*

| *Deductible* | | *Annual Premium* |
|---|---|---|
| None | = | $70 |
| $50 | = | $50 |
| $100 | = | $30 |
| $200 | = | $20 |

Using the above table as a guide, you could raise the comprehensive deductible from none at all to $100 and thereby save $40 a year. Notice that there is very little difference in cost between the $100 deductible and the $200 deductible.

6. For those who itemize their deductions on their tax returns, it is interesting to note

that uninsured casualty losses (comprehensive, collision, and homeowner's losses) over a $100 threshold are tax deductible. For example, if you suffered a $1,000 collision loss and claimed it under your $500 deductible auto insurance policy, the insurance company would pay $500 of the loss. Then you would be allowed to deduct $400 of the uninsured amount ($500 uninsured amount − $100 threshold = $400 itemized deduction) on your tax return. If you didn't carry the collision coverage, you could deduct $900 of the total loss ($1,000 collision loss − $100 threshold = $900 itemized deduction).

In effect, if you itemize your tax return and have the comprehensive or collision deductibles set higher than $100, or if you don't carry these coverages at all, Uncle Sam will help you pay for part of any casualty loss over the $100 threshold amount.

## Limits of Liability, Uninsured Motorist Coverage, No-Fault and Medical Payments Coverages

Stated quite simply, the liability portion of your auto insurance policy pays for all judgments in lawsuits you are obligated to pay as a result of your negligence in an auto accident. It will also pay for the bodily injuries or death to others, as well as for the damages to, destruction of, or loss of use of property of others up to the limits of your coverages. For example, if you have the minimum liability limits of 10/20/5, your policy will pay up to $10,000 to each person you injure or who dies in an auto accident, but will pay no more than $20,000 for all injured or deceased persons in that same accident. In addition, your policy would pay up to $5,000 for all the damage you may cause to the property of others. The rates for this very important coverage are approximately as follows:

| *Limits of Liability* | *Annual Premium Amounts* |
|---|---|
| 10/20/5 | $130 |
| 25/50/25 | $144 |
| 50/100/50 | $160 |
| 100/300/50 | $170 |

Uninsured motorist coverage would pay you for your injuries (bodily injuries only) caused by negligent uninsured motorists up to the limits of your coverage. For example, if you have the minimum limits of 10/20, an injured party would be covered for up to $10,000, but all injured parties couldn't collect more than

$20,000 combined. The rates for this important coverage are approximately as follows:

| *Uninsured Motorist Coverage Amounts* | *Annual Premium Amounts* |
|---|---|
| 10/20 | $4 |
| 25/50 | $8 |
| 50/100 | $15 |
| 100/300 | $20 |

It is my opinion that your auto policy should be allowed to perform as it was intended to, that is, to provide adequate liability protection in the event of an adverse lawsuit. In fact, to do otherwise is comparable to making a bad bet that, if lost, could mean the forfeiture of one's home and property or even the garnishment of one's future earnings. A casual glance of the preceding premium tables should make you realize that carrying the lower liability coverages is not only a bad gamble but a downright foolish act, since the higher limits of liability are available for only a few extra dollars a year. For example, a raise from the minimum 10/20/5 to 25/50/25 is only about 14 extra dollars a year! A raise to 50/100/50 would only cost an extra $30, while a raise to the pinnacle of 100/300/50 would cost an extra $40 a year. It is worth paying the few extra dollars for the higher liability protection, and I recommend that you have this important matter taken care of the next time you call your insurance representative.

Once your liability limits have been set at their most realistic levels, it makes sense to protect yourself and your family with adequate uninsured motorist coverage. The U.M. coverage is designed to pay you for your injuries inflicted by uninsured and/or underinsured motorists. For example, if you were an accident victim and were awarded $100,000 from the court, the 100/300 uninsured motorist coverage would pay all of that amount if the guilty party hit and ran, didn't have insurance, or had the bare minimum limits of liability and no other assets.

I believe U.M. coverage is the least expensive disability payment protection you can buy. The cost difference between the minimum coverage of 10/20 and the maximum amount of 100/300 is only $16 a year. It doesn't make sense not to take advantage of this very important coverage.

When you understand the makeup of your rate classification and the factors that affect it, you can make the appropriate adjustments to lower your premium while using a small portion of your savings to increase the vital liability and uninsured motorist coverages, which will substantially enhance your overall insurance protection at the expense of the insurance company. For example, if Sections A–I of this book have enabled you to save $180 a year, you easily could take $40 of it and raise your liability limits to 100/300/50 and then take another $16 to raise the uninsured motorist protection to its maximum of 100/300 and still pocket $124 a year! It makes sense to have your coverages work harder for you.

Although the liability and uninsured motorist coverages are very important, so are the medical payments and the no-fault (personal injury protection) coverages. The medical payments coverage should be purchased if no-fault isn't offered in your state.

Simply explained, the medical payments coverage will pay the medical expenses or funeral bills of the insured or the insured's live-in relatives up to the limits of the selected coverage—from $5,000 to $100,000 per person. The insured and the insured's live-in relatives are covered while driving or being driven in the car; the insured would be covered if struck by a vehicle as a pedestrian or as a bicyclist. I definitely recommend that you purchase the maximum coverage that's available in your state because the extra cost would only amount to $6–$10 a year.

If you live in a no-fault state, you could be covered from a minimum of $5,000 to a maximum of $100,000, which, again, would only cost a few extra dollars a year. In simple language, no-fault was created to reduce the number of bodily injury lawsuits that were cluttering the courts years ago and was instituted to accelerate the payment of bodily injury claims regardless of who was at fault. Essentially, no-fault provides the same benefits as medical payments coverage, and also provides compensation for lost wages—from 75 to 100 percent of one's weekly salary up to $200 a week for a maximum of 52 weeks; compensation for additional household chores and services paying up to $25 a day, but for no longer than 365 days, and a survivor's income benefit paying up to $2,000 as a result of any insured's death in an auto accident.

In most cases, the preceding coverages follow the insured's car, which would be covered while being driven anywhere in the United States, Canada, or any of their provinces or possessions. It's important to note that if American drivers took their cars with them while vacationing in Mexico, South America, Europe, or the Far East, their insurance would cease to apply in those foreign areas and they would have to purchase the car insurance of those countries which, in fact, is very similar to our own. All of this can be easily avoided if you rent a car while vacationing in foreign countries. You would obtain essentially the same coverage and protection we receive on rentals in the States.

Note that if you drive a borrowed car, a rented car, or a company car, the insurance on those vehicles acts as primary coverage while your individual policy would give you secondary coverage where and if needed.

For those who had the wisdom to choose the highest levels of coverage on all of their personal liability-type policies—auto 100/300/50, homeowner's or renter's $100,000, and aircraft or boat 100/300/50, etc.—they can now more adequately protect themselves from today's extravagant judgments with an umbrella policy, which gives an additional $1 million of protection. For example, if someone slipped on a banana peel while strolling on your sidewalk and was injured and awarded $500,000, your homeowner's policy would pay the first $100,000 while the umbrella policy would pay the remaining $400,000 and literally save the day.

Insurance companies require their prospective umbrella liability policyholders to carry the highest limits of personal liability either with the company that offers this type of coverage or with some other insurance company. In most cases, definite proof is required, such as the submission of your other policy's declaration pages (Dec Pages), or some other written proof or statement from the client or insurance representative. Since the premium for this miracle personal liability umbrella policy is only about $90 a year, I not only recommend it, but urge you to call your agent/broker so that you can take advantage of it today.

**States with No-Fault Coverage**

| | | |
|---|---|---|
| Colorado | Kansas | New Jersey |
| Connecticut | Kentucky | New York |
| Florida | Massachusetts | North Dakota |
| Georgia | Michigan | Pennsylvania |
| Hawaii | Minnesota | Utah |

## States with Minimum Liability Limits (Compulsory* or Noncompulsory)

| *State or Possession* | *Minimum Liability Limits* | *State or Possession* | *Minimum Liability Limits* |
|---|---|---|---|
| Alabama | 10/20/5 | Nebraska | 15/30/10 |
| Alaska | 25/50/10 | Nevada* | 15/30/5 |
| Arizona | 15/30/10 | New Hampshire | 20/40/5 |
| Arkansas | 25/25/15 | New Jersey* | 15/30/5 |
| California* | 15/30/5 | New Mexico | 15/30/5 |
| Colorado* | 15/30/5 | New York* | 10/20/5 |
| Connecticut* | 20/40/5 | North Carolina* | 25/50/10 |
| Delaware* | 10/20/5 | North Dakota* | 25/50/10 |
| District of Columbia | 10/20/5 | Ohio | 12.5/25/7.5 |
| Florida | 10/20/5 | Oklahoma* | 10/20/10 |
| Georgia* | 20/30/5 | Oregon* | 15/30/5 |
| Hawaii* | 25/unlimited/10 | Pennsylvania* | 15/30/5 |
| Idaho* | 10/20/5 | Puerto Rico | no provision |
| Illinois | 15/30/10 | Rhode Island | 25/50/10 |
| Indiana | 15/30/10 | South Carolina* | 15/30/5 |
| Iowa | 15/30/10 | South Dakota | 15/30/10 |
| Kansas* | 25/50/10 | Tennessee | 10/20/5 |
| Kentucky* | 10/20/5 | Texas | 10/30/5 |
| Louisiana* | 5/10/1 | Utah* | 15/30/5 |
| Maine | 20/40/10 | Vermont | 20/40/10 |
| Maryland* | 10/40/10 | Virginia | 25/50/10 |
| Massachusetts* | 10/20/5 | Virgin Islands* | 10/20/10 |
| Michigan* | 20/40/10 | Washington | 25/50/10 |
| Minnesota* | 25/50/10 | West Virginia | 20/40/10 |
| Mississippi | 10/20/5 | Wisconsin | 15/30/10 |
| Missouri | 10/20/2 | Wyoming* | 10/20/5 |
| Montana* | 25/50/5 | | |

# 2

# The Youthful Driver—How to Get the Affordable Rate

Because the nonprincipal operator classification, multi-car discount, driver training discount, and good student credit are at the heart of getting an affordable rate for the young driver, I would like to examine them before going on to other premium-reducing strategies.

## The Nonprincipal Operator Classification

First, if you live at home and your parents allow you to be added to their policy, you could cancel your individual insurance and have your classification changed from a principal operator to a nonprincipal operator. A nonprincipal operator doesn't own a car and, as an occasional driver, puts on less than 25 percent of the total mileage—except in New York, Pennsylvania, and South Carolina, which are the only states that allow nonprincipal operators to drive up to 50 percent of the total mileage.

### The Multi-Car, Driver Training, and Good Student Discounts

You can save up to 35 percent a year simply by lowering your driving mileage to meet your state's requirements and by registering the car in your parent's name. This is without even allowing for the multi-car discount (two or more vehicles insured on the same policy), which can save both you and your parents another 20 percent! In addition, driver training and good student discounts (maintaining at least a B grade average) are available in all states and can save you another 5–10 percent if you're under age 21.

For instance, if you're a single male under age 21 living at home and make the above adjustments, instead of facing a \$720 or \$1,080 principal operator rate, you could pay as little as \$374 (\$720 × .65 nonprincipal operator credit = \$468 × .80 multi-car discount = \$374) for a 48 percent savings. The driver training or good student discounts could lower the \$374 premium by another 5–10 percent depending upon your situation and individual company policy. As a single male under age 21, you can approximate your potential savings simply by cutting your present rate in half and then allowing for driver training or good student discounts where applicable. After meeting the above requirements, your parents can make arrangements with their insurance representative while you can reimburse them for your portion of the total premium bill.

Single males between the ages of 21 and 24 who meet the nonprincipal driver requirements can have their rates lowered from their previous high range of $630 to $810 to as little as $328 ($630 × .65 nonprincipal operator credit = $410 × .80 multi-car discount = $328). Single males between the ages of 21 and 24 can estimate their savings by cutting their present rates in half if they make the preceding nonprincipal operator adjustments.

Single males between the ages of 25 and 29 are not permitted the nonprincipal operator classification. However, if they still live at home with their parents, they can be added to their family policy as extra drivers and receive the benefit of the 20 percent multi-car discount. In this case, the $450 rate for single males aged 25–29 could be reduced to $360 ($450 × .80 multi-car discount = $360). However, if you live in your own home and have your own policy, you can still lower your bill in various ways that I will discuss later.

Single females under age 21 who meet their state's nonprincipal operator requirements can have their rates lowered from the $630–$810 range to as little as $328 ($630 × .65 nonprincipal operator credit = $410 × .80 multi-car discount = $328.00) for a 48 percent savings. The driver training and good student discounts could further reduce the above rate by another 5–10 percent where applicable.

Single females between the ages of 21–24 who meet the nonprincipal operator requirements can have their rates lowered from the $504–$630 range to as little as $262 ($504 × .65 nonprincipal operator credit = $328 × .80 multi-car discount = $262) for another 48 percent savings. The driver training and good student discounts are not available for those who are 21 and older.

You can qualify for the nonprincipal operator credit if you're a student under the age of 25, living at home and attending a local school or college. You would also qualify if you moved to a distant college, left the car at home, and used it only during summer vacations and holiday visits. But remember that you would not qualify for the credit if you moved to a distant college and took the car with you. In this case, you could still be added to your parents' policy and receive the multi-car discount, but would be rated as a principal operator with the resultant higher premiums. The following table shows the rates you could expect in this case:

**Single Males**

| | | |
|---|---|---|
| less than 21 | $576 | ($720 × .80) |
| ages 21–24 | $504 | ($630 × .80) |
| ages 25–29 | $360 | ($450 × .80) |

**Single Females**

| | | |
|---|---|---|
| less than 21 | $504 | ($630 × .80) |
| ages 21–24 | $403 | ($504 × .80) |
| ages 25 + | $288 | ($360 × .80) |

Another important point to remember is that once added to your parents' policy, you are obligated to drive extra cautiously, since your speeding tickets, moving violations, and at-fault accidents affect not only your own rate, but that of your parents as well. For example, if a 21-year-old male lived at home with his parents, who owned two average-priced five-year-old cars, the annual insurance premium would approximate $662 ($288 for the parents and $374 for the son). But if the son caused an accident, the total insurance bill could be surcharged by as much as 20 percent, which would produce a final premium of $795 ($346 for the parents and $449 for the son). A second at-fault accident in a three-year period would add another 20 percent to the total bill, increasing the final premium to $954. The rate hike would continue for each additional accident.

A simple speeding ticket or moving violation could raise the rates of everyone covered by 10 percent per infraction. For example, if a son received a speeding ticket within a three-year period, the total premium could be raised to $728 ($317 for the parents and $411 for the son). Another infraction within a three-year period could raise the rates by another 10 percent, an at-fault accident could raise the already inflated premium by another 20 percent, and so on. As you can see, it pays to drive cautiously when you are added on to your parents' policy.

Parents should be aware that they are entitled to a rate break once their children permanently move from their households. Children's speeding tickets, moving violations, and accidents will follow them from the home and will no longer affect the parents' rates. Therefore, parents should call their representative immediately for a rate reduction once a child moves out on his or her own. However, if they have forgotten to do this in the past, they may be entitled not only to an immediate rate reduction *but also to a premium refund for their past overcharges.*

For example, if you are a parent who was paying a $700 annual premium because of a son or daughter living at home and you failed to notify your insurance representative when he or she moved out a year ago, you would be entitled to an immediate premium reduction to $300 plus a $400 premium refund check for that year. If the move occurred two years ago, you would be entitled to an $800 refund check and so on, up to your state's statute of limitations, which is usually seven years.

Of course, you would have to produce documents and other evidence proving the permanence of the move—rent receipts, paycheck stubs, etc. But it would be worth the effort. In fact, most insurance companies will cooperate with you and redeem what is rightfully yours. However, if you feel that your company is procrastinating or if it refuses to pay your claim, don't hesitate to call or write your state insurance department consumer affairs division, which will investigate your case. If your claim is deemed legitimate, they will force your company to pay the refund promptly.

Your other option is to take your case to a small-claims court or to a lawyer, but chances are good that your complaint can be settled with the help of your state insurance department. See sample letters G and H.

## SAMPLE LETTER G

Requesting the reduction of your auto insurance premium and the remittance of your refund check.

9/20/81

John/Jane Policyholder
110 Washington Ave.
Anywhere, U.S.A.
Policy # 60-475-120-89

A.B.C. Insurance Company
250 State St.
Anywhere, U.S.A.

Dear A.B.C. Insurance Company:

A year ago, my twenty-one-year-old son left my household permanently and joined the service. However, I understand that your records are still showing him residing with me, which of course is in error.

After discussing this with my agent/broker,

I realized that my previous year's rates didn't reflect the fact that he had left my home and that my premium should have been substantially reduced at that time.

Therefore, my agent/broker requested that my premium be reduced from $700 a year to $300 and that I be sent a refund check for $400 as reimbursement for last year's overpayment.

In cooperation with my agent/broker, I've enclosed a photocopy of my son's service record to assist you with the prompt reduction of my premium and to support the timely remittance of my refund check.

I thank you for your immediate attention and full cooperation in this matter.

Sincerely,
John/Jane Policyholder

## SAMPLE LETTER H

Requesting your state insurance department to assist you with the refund check.

10/21/81

John/Jane Policyholder
110 Washington Ave.
Anywhere, U.S.A.
Policy # 60-475-120-89

State Insurance Department
Division of Consumer Affairs
100 Capitol St.
Anystate, U.S.A.

Dear Insurance Department:

I enclose a copy of my letter dated 9/20/81, which I sent to the A.B.C. Insurance Company requesting the reduction of my auto insurance premium and the timely remittance of my refund check. I also enclose a copy of my son's service record that I referred to in my letter.

Although the A.B.C. Insurance Company reduced my premium from $700 to $300 a year, I still haven't received my $400 refund check. Therefore, I request your immediate assistance in lieu of my taking this to a small-claims court, my giving this to my attorney for additional action, or my taking this up with my congressman.

Please contact me as soon as possible so that this urgent matter can be settled promptly.

Again, I thank you for your timely assistance.

Sincerely,
John/Jane Policyholder

cc: A.B.C. Insurance Company

## Other Valuable Saving Tips

In addition to getting the nonprincipal operator classification, multi-car discount, driver training, and good student discounts, there are several other premium saving strategies of which you should be aware.

If you must have your own insurance policy, your first car should be a standard performance vehicle and *not* a sports car or a modified hot rod. In addition to the fact that the comprehensive and collision coverages will be twice the normal rates, many insurance companies simply will not accept the added risk of covering such vehicles and you could find yourself needlessly in the assigned risk pool. For example, if your rate factor was 2.00 and you had a choice between owning a standard performance vehicle and a sports car, the physical damage premium would be almost double the standard annual amount—$440 versus only $240.

However, if you insist on owning a sports model, the smart thing to do is to start off with a standard performance vehicle. Once you're officially accepted by the company (sixty or more days of coverage), and given an insurance policy, you could then switch over to the type of car you originally had in mind. Don't forget that if you must carry the physical damage coverages, that portion of your premium will definitely shoot up. However, if you don't carry the comprehensive and collision coverages at this time, there are no differences between the rates for owning the different types of car.

In most cases, after sixty days, the insurance company will have to keep insuring you for at least three years. After that it could cancel your policy for driving an unacceptable vehicle.

Another point to remember is that when adding a youthful driver to the parents' policy, try to have the son or daughter rated on the oldest or least valuable vehicle. In addition to the nonprincipal operator savings and the other related discounts previously mentioned, this adjustment will save a family at least another 10 percent and sometimes even more. In a two-car family with an 18-year-old son who occasionally drives, there would be a big difference in the final premium if he was rated on the 1973 clunker rather than on the 1981 Grand Ritz.

If, on the other hand, the son were rated on the 1973 clunker while the parents were rated on their 1981 Grand Ritz, the final annual premium would be $596 or $96 less for an additional 14 percent savings.

| | *1981 Grand Ritz with son rated as nonprincipal driver* | *1973 clunker with parents rated as principal drivers* |
|---|---|---|
| Bodily injury and property damage liability 50/100/50 | $160.00 | $160.00 |
| Medical payments or no-fault | 28.00 | 28.00 |
| Uninsured motorist | 2.00 | 2.00 |
| Collision—$200 deductible | 60.00 | |
| Comprehensive—$50 deductible | 20.00 | |
| Annual base premium | $270.00 | $190.00 |
| Times rating factor | × 2.00 | × .80 |
| Annual premiums | $540.00 | $152.00 |

Total Annual premium = $692.00 ($540.00 + $152.00)

| | *1981 Grand Ritz with parents rated as principal drivers* | *1973 clunker with son rated as nonprincipal driver* |
|---|---|---|
| Annual base premium | $270.00 | $190.00 |
| Times rating factor | × .80 | × 2.00 |
| Annual premiums | $216.00 | $380.00 |

Total annual premium = $596.00 ($216.00 + $380.00)

The preceding rating method saved an additional 14 percent on top of the nonprincipal operator credit, multi-car discount, driver training and good student discounts, which in themselves saved this youthful driver and his family well over 50 percent.

Another important point to remember is that if you're a young newlywed couple under age 25, you could both save a lot of premium dollars just by registering and insuring the car in the wife's name, since married males under age 25 have a rating factor anywhere from 15–50 percent higher than that of their spouse. For example, a newlywed couple who are both age 21 and own a moderately priced car can save approximately $108 a year for the next four years by registering and insuring their car under her name ($468 premium for married males aged 21 – $360 premium for married females at any age = $108 annual savings or $432 over four years). Once the husband reaches age 25, it wouldn't matter in whose name the car is registered, since married males age 25 and older have the same low rating factor as their wives. In this example, the husband's premium would also be $360 when he turns age 25.

Finally, young single females receive far better treatment at the hands of the insurance companies than their single male counterparts. Therefore, I suggest that the females review the premium saving techniques in Chapter 1 and, in particular, the section on Age, Sex, and Marital Status.

# 3.

# Learning the Rules—The Art of Keeping a Low Rate

## The Benefits of Maintaining a Clean Driving Record

Since no one wants to be forced into paying more than necessary for car insurance, it is vitally important to have and maintain a perfect or near perfect (no more than a total of one at-fault accident or one moving violation) driving record over each three to five years. Most insurance companies judge your driving record over a three-year period, but there are a few that still use a five-year time frame. As you'll see in Chapter 5, I think this is unnecessarily harsh and a bad deal for policyholders.

## How to Avoid and Successfully Contest the Speeding Ticket

There are many commonsense precautions you can take to prevent yourself from being ticketed or charged with an accident. You can be more alert near the well-known speed trap areas or use a CB radio to bird-dog the hidden speed traps. But simply slowing down and driving cautiously for your own safety as well as that of others is really the best tactic of all. Whenever you're in a hurry or in a gambling mood, keep in mind that if you are caught the citation can cause havoc with your car insurance premium as well as destroy your chances of getting a better deal elsewhere.

If you are wrongfully charged with a speeding ticket or traffic violation, you can contest it in court, especially if you have favorable witnesses or other legal grounds to prove your case. Although it's feasible to fight your own case, your chances of winning increase immensely the moment you hire legal counsel. Legal fees can range from \$50 to \$200, which can be quite a bargain when compared to potential premium penalties over the next three to five years. For example, if you're currently paying a \$500 annual premium and at the same time are facing a four-point moving violation, your premium rate could be increased by as much as 20 percent over the next three to five years. This would result in a \$600 annual rate—a \$300 to \$500 premium penalty (\$500 × .20 = \$100 × 3 years = \$300 or × 5 years

= \$500). It is certainly worth the legal fees to win such a case, not only for the near-term premium savings but also for the added bonus of maintaining a clean driving record for future policy price shopping.

## How to Prove Your Innocence in Traffic Accidents

Beating a speeding ticket is a piece of cake when compared to proving your innocence in an accident. Most states have contributory negligence laws on their books that compel each party to prove his or her freedom from contributing to the accident in addition to proving the full negligence of the other party—which isn't very easy these days. Therefore, most states allow the insurance companies to substantially raise your rates (.40 surcharge to the rating factor per accident in New York State, for instance), unless you can prove that the other driver or drivers were fully at fault and thereby caused the accident. If you're involved in an accident, you're already guilty in the eyes of the insurance company unless you can prove your innocence at the accident scene or subsequently in a court of law.

This is a very important area of car insurance savings, since a .40 rate surcharge can increase your final premium anywhere from 10–50 percent over the next three to five years, depending upon your insurance company's policy and your present rate factor. The lower your rate factor, the greater the surcharge impact. If your rate factor is 1.00, with an annual premium of $500, a chargeable at-fault accident would raise your rate factor from 1.00 to 1.40 and surcharge your premium by 40 percent to $700 for the next three to five years. This disastrous situation would cost you anywhere from $600 to $1,000 of additional premium dollars!

Therefore, in order to overcome this legal gauntlet and the surcharge penalty, you need to know several important principles to keep in mind if involved in an accident:

1. Keep a cool head and memorize the license plate number of the other vehicle(s) just in case the driver(s) flees the accident scene. Call or have someone phone the police and, if necessary, the ambulance. Also, if possible, try to protect yourself, the other parties, and your car from further damage.

2. Try to gather as many third-party witnesses as possible because your passengers will not be as credible as disinterested third-party witnesses. They, in most cases, are the only

ones able to prove your innocence at the accident scene or later in court. Be sure to write down the names, addresses, and telephone numbers of all available witnesses.

3. Once the police arrive, fill out the accident report while exchanging the following vital information: names, addresses, telephone and license numbers of each driver, plus those of their passengers; license plate numbers, year, make, and model of each car plus the owner's name, address, and telephone number; and the name, address, and telephone numbers of their insurance company(s) and representatives.

4. At this point, arrange to have your witnesses testify to the police on your behalf, especially if the other driver(s) committed a moving violation or caused the accident in any way. After your witnesses submit their favorable testimony, be very insistent that the police log the evidence in the accident report and strongly request that the offender(s) be cited on the spot for their moving violations and charged with the accident. With this above information properly logged in the accident report, you'll be completely exonerated from any negligence and will be in a position to collect fully (no

deductible) from the guilty party's insurance company. Ask for a copy of the accident report or determine where and when it can be obtained so that with the preceding information you'll be fully prepared for any future court action.

5. As a precaution and while everything is still fresh in your mind, take a few moments to write down all the details of the accident including the time, date, weather, and road conditions; a diagram of the accident scene showing the position and direction of your car before and after being struck; and a description of how the offender's moving violation caused the accident.

6. Call your insurance representative and give him or her all the pertinent information so that you can be given the proper advice and assistance with your claim against the other driver's insurance company.

Proving one's innocence in an accident with the aid of cooperative third party witnesses is quite easy when compared to being involved in an accident with no available witnesses. Without witnesses many safe drivers find themselves charged with accidents they didn't cause for the simple reason that they did not know how to go about proving their innocence. Therefore, I suggest the following steps whenever involved in an accident where favorable witnesses are not available:

1. Again, keep a cool head and memorize the license plate of the other vehicle(s) just in case the driver(s) flee the accident scene. Call or have someone phone the police and, if necessary, the ambulance. Also, if possible, try to protect yourself, the other parties, and your car from further damage.

2. Take the instant print camera (which you should keep handy for situations like this) and take shots of the accident scene including skid marks, location of both vehicles, and debris. Try to prove your case with the shots so that when the police arrive, you'll have *prima facie* evidence to support your case. The police will be impressed, and you'll have a psychological edge over your opponent, which usually compels the guilty party to make admissions that they wouldn't otherwise make.

   If you convince the police of your innocence, be very insistent that the evidence is logged in the accident report while strongly requesting that the offender(s) be cited on the spot for their moving violations and charged with the accident.

3. Complete the accident report and exchange the following vital information: name, addresses, telephone and license numbers of each driver plus those of their passengers; license plate numbers, year, make, and model of each car plus the owner's name, address, and telephone number; and the name, address, and telephone numbers of their insurance company(s) and representatives.

4. As a precaution and while everything is still fresh in your mind, take a few moments to write down all the details of the accident including the time, date, weather, and road conditions; a diagram of the accident scene showing the position and direction of your car before and after being struck; and a description of how the offender's moving violation caused the accident.

5. Call your insurance representative and fill him or her in on all the above details. Hang on to those pictures, since they can be admitted as evidence in any future court action. Repair the damage to your car and send the bill to the other insurance com-

pany. If a problem arises, have an attorney send the company a letter outlining the claim.

## How to Avoid Premium Surcharges and Rate Hike Penalties

Unfortunately, not everyone is a perfect driver. Someday you may find yourself causing or contributing to an accident. In all states except New York, where it was recently raised to $400, the submission of small collision claims of under $300 will not cause the insurance company to surcharge your rate and your future premiums will not be affected. However, in all states except New York, small claims of over $300 will activate the premium surcharge penalty. In such cases, it would be wiser to pay for the damages out of your pocket rather than face the .40 surcharge penalty for the next three to five years.

For example, if your current premium is $500 and you accidentally back your car into a tree, causing $450 damage, you would be far better off paying that collision claim out of your pocket than presenting it to your insurance company, which would surcharge your rate by raising it to $700 for each of the next three to five years ($500 original rate × 1.40 = $700).

The submission of this claim would force you to pay anywhere from $600 to $1,000 more in a premium ($200 surcharge × 3 or 5 years), which is far more than the original $450 claim.

On the other hand, if your damages are greater than the imminent surcharge of $600 to $1,000, it would make more sense to submit the claim and pay the extra premium over the next three to five years. If the damage amounted to $2,000 and your collision deductible was set at $200, you would collect $1,800 under your claim while being assessed a surcharge for the next three to five years. You would still be ahead of the game by anywhere from $1,200 ($1,800 reimbursement – $600 surcharge) to $800 ($1,800 reimbursement – $1,000 surcharge). But keep in mind that you would then have a chargeable accident against your driving record, which would limit your policy shopping activities to a few of the more liberal insurance companies.

In summary, it is currently safe to submit accident claims of under $300 in all states except New York, where small claims was raised to $400, because these amounts are below your state's chargeable accident threshold level and will not activate the premium surcharge penalty. To be absolutely sure that your collision claim will not result in a premium surcharge, before submitting the claim, call your insurance representative or state insurance department to verify the chargeable accident threshold amount that is currently applicable in your state.

For collision claims of over $300 ($400 in New York), be sure to compare the amount of your claim to the sum total of the impending yearly surcharges. If your claim amount is greater than the impending premium in creases, submit it. If the claim amount is less, you would be better off taking care of the damage yourself. Call your insurance representative for help when making this decision.

# 4

# How to Recognize a Good Car Insurance Deal

Contrary to popular thinking, the differences in the rate structures among the various insurance companies are so huge that blindly staying with the same company year after year rarely puts one on the stairway to heaven. In many cases, however, to do so can put one on an escalator to higher than usual premiums.

If an insurance company experiences extraordinary losses, they are usually passed on to policyholders in the form of higher rates and stricter penalties. Since auto insurance companies don't widely publicize their loss ratios, a policyholder has no way of knowing except through his or her state insurance departments if this is the case.

It stands to reason that safe drivers of any insurance company should not be overly penalized for the transgressions of their fellow policyholders. In fact, since it is tough enough to maintain a good driving record, there is no reason why any safe driver should have to pay excessive premiums for his or her own insurance company's underwriting mistakes.

## How to Avoid Car Insurance Rip-offs and Exorbitant Rates

It is difficult to understand why, in many cases, customer loyalty is rewarded only with higher rates at each renewal period; it is even more difficult to understand why these policyholders shrug it off in the false belief that everyone is receiving the same treatment. They fail to realize that they could be getting a better deal practically anywhere else.

Fortunately, there are many fine insurance companies with excellent rate structures to choose from. The following guidelines will help you clear up any questions regarding your present situation and give you direction in making future changes:

1. Other than the assigned risk plan, it is not the usual practice of insurance companies to raise rates for the occasional moving violation that doesn't result in an at-fault accident. If your present company raised your premium or makes a practice of surcharg-

ing or severely penalizing its policyholders for the occasional moving violation, it would probably be to your advantage to switch to a more lenient company.

For example, if you had a clean driving record for years but were recently cited for overlooking a newly placed "yield" sign which prompted your company to raise your premium by 10 percent from $280 a year to $308, it would definitely be to your advantage to switch over to one of the more lenient companies that would return you to your original $280 rate. This move would not only give you immediate satisfaction but also future peace of mind, since you will be dealing with a more tolerant and open-minded company, not to mention the 10 percent annual premium savings.

2. Many fine insurance companies have a policy of not penalizing policyholders for accidents that result in damages only to the insured's vehicle—for example, skidding off the road and striking a snowbank while not inflicting bodily injury or causing property damage to other third parties. If you were penalized by your insurance company for this type of accident, it would pay you to find a more lenient company. The premium

savings would be quite substantial—up to .40 off the rating factor.

If you skidded on an oil slick, striking an old tree stump, and put in a claim for which your company surcharged your rate by .40, raising it from $350 to $490, you would be more than justified in finding a more lenient company that would return your premium to its original $350 level or maybe even less. The switch would probably save you every bit of the potential three-year surcharge of $420 that you would otherwise have to pay.

3. Most insurance companies have a standard policy of not surcharging their policyholders for accidents caused by hit-and-run drivers, or when struck while legally parked. In fact, some companies overlook accidents that result from the insured's conscientious efforts to avoid children darting into the street or from avoiding other serious types of accidents.

4. Other than the assigned risk plan, many companies count a simultaneous moving violation and a resulting accident as only one chargeable incident. If you were charged separately for both the moving violation and the resulting accident, it would be wise to change to a company that would only

charge you once for such an accident. The change would save you anywhere from 10–20 percent, since you wouldn't be penalized for the moving violation.

For example, if prior to an accident your premium was $300 a year and it was subsequently surcharged by .40 to $420 for the chargeable accident, then raised again by another .20 to $480 for the moving violation, you should find a replacement company that would charge only $420 over the next three to five years. This switch would save you at least $180.

5. Insurance rates should not be affected by minor accidents in which your company pays claims that are less than your state's chargeable accident threshold amount—less than $400 in New York and less than $300 in the remaining states. If your rates were surcharged as a result of a minor accident that caused less damage than your state's threshold amount, you were given a very bad deal and should definitely shop around for a better company.

   For example, if you were involved in an accident and your company paid you, or some other party on account of you, a total amount of less than your state's chargeable accident threshold level, there would be no justification for it to surcharge your premium. If the company went ahead and surcharged your rate anyway, you could simply walk away and take your business to a more fair-minded company.

6. In most cases, senior citizen rates for drivers 65 and older should be about 10 percent less than the standard adult/married rate. Under no circumstances should senior citizens be penalized or thrown into the assigned risk pool simply because of their age. In fact, other than a bad driving record or a severe physical impairment, senior citizens may shop around for a better deal just like anyone else. For example, if the standard adult/married rate for a medium-priced car was \$360 a year, the senior citizen rate should be approximately \$324 (\$360 × .90). A senior citizen paying more than the preceding amount should, barring a poor driving record or a severe physical handicap, shop around for a better deal and save the \$36-a-year difference.

7. If your company has a stringent policy of penalizing or surcharging its policyholders over a five-year period rather than the usual three-year period, it would make more

sense to switch companies, especially if your rate is currently being surcharged and approaching the third-year mark.

For example, if you've been assessed a .40 surcharge over the past three years that raised your premium from $300 to $420 and your company intends to maintain that surcharged rate for another two years, it would benefit you to change to a company with a three-year assessment period, freeing yourself from that unnecessary surcharge and regaining your original $300 rate. This change would save you $240 over the next two years, plus giving you added peace of mind.

8. It's an unfair policy for an insurance company to match and rate youthful drivers to the newest and most expensive vehicles in their family households rather than to the older cars that they usually drive. For example, if you're a family man with a seventeen-year-old son whose individual insurance rate is based upon your new car and not on the older vehicle that you bought him, it is probably costing you an additional 10–20 percent premium every year. If you're paying $600 a year based upon the above rating process, you could easily have your rate re-

duced to anywhere from $540 to $480 a year simply by shopping for a company with a more realistic rating policy.

9. If you or your family members maintained a clean driving record over the past three or more years, check to see if your insurance bill or policy declaration page (the one that shows all the coverages) indicates that you have been receiving the good driver discount or the accident-free rate. If you do not see it indicated, call your insurance representative and find out why, since the discount could already be included in your rate but not shown. In a simple case of home office oversight, you're entitled to the lower rate plus an additional refund for the past overcharges. If your insurance company doesn't provide these valuable discounts, you could save yourself another 5–10 percent by shopping around for a company that issues them.

## How to Choose the Best Insurance Representative

It is very important to have a competent and sincere insurance representative because his or her judgment will have a lot to do with the quality of service you receive and the price you pay for it.

Insurance *agents* represent the companies that employ them; insurance *brokers* represent their clients with a variety of insurance companies. At first glance, it may appear that the brokers have a distinct advantage over their agent competitors, but that is not always true because agents can be as, or even more, price competitive than brokers. In the final analysis, it boils down to choosing the one person who is willing to work his or her hardest to give you the finest service for the least amount of premium. Sometimes it will be an agent; other times, a broker. It all depends upon that person's professionalism and ability to be price competitive.

When shopping around, either as a price-conscious consumer, a person who just relocated to a new area, or a newly licensed driver, your first step is to take the advice of friends, neighbors, relatives, or business associates so that you'll have a list of recommended companies when working with the "Car Insurance Comparison Chart." (See Chapter 5.)

# 5

# Shopping Around—On the Road to Lower Rates

During your driving lifetime, you'll probably be changing insurance companies several times. The guidelines found in this chapter will be instrumental to your pursuit of low-cost car insurance and should be remembered when shopping around and comparing premiums.

## The Art of Finding the Rock-Bottom Rates

To save a lot of time and effort, make sure that all the drivers and all of the vehicles in your household meet the prospective companies' minimum underwriting requirements. You can accomplish this by knowing your own driving record as well as those of the other members of your household. If in doubt, you can verify this through your local department of motor vehicles. Once that's achieved, make a number of phone calls to the various insurance companies or their agents/brokers in your local area and ask each one of them for their driving record and vehicle-type requirements.

After several calls, you'll discover that the minimum driving record requirements usually demand no more than either one chargeable accident or no more than one moving violation per person or per family over a three-year period. You may discover that there are a number of companies that require an absolutely clean record for all persons they initially insure. But don't be taken back by all of this because, as a rule of thumb, the stricter the underwriting requirements, the lower the rates.

Seek the advice of friends, neighbors, relatives, or business associates when narrowing down your list of potential insurers because their many years of firsthand experience with these insurance companies can be quite illuminating.

In order to ensure that you're getting the lowest quotes, make the prospective insurers fully aware of the premium saving changes and adjustments you have made as a result of the recommendations in the previous chapters—for example, you are now taking public transportation or are car pooling to work so that your driving usage category is at its lowest; pleasure use, including driving to work, less than 30 round-trip miles per week; you now leave your newest car at home and take the older one without the comprehensive and collision coverages to work; you're raising the amount of the collision deductible on all your vehicles; you now drive less than 7,500 miles per year because of out-of-sight gas prices; the accident you had two years ago was not your fault and you can prove it; and your teenagers are occasional drivers who operate their clunkers exclusively and should be rated only on those cars.

Also, make the prospective insurers fully aware of all the discounts you're entitled to: the multi-car discount, the safe driver or accident-free discount, the nonprincipal operator discount for youthful drivers and the driver training and good student discounts, the low mileage discount, the pleasure use discount, etc.

Obtain at least a half dozen quotes before narrowing your list down to a few selected companies. See the Car Insurance Comparison Chart on the following two pages.

Make sure that you are fully accepted at the rate quoted and are given a binder (contractual

**Car Insurance Comparison Chart**

| *Present company & coverages* | *Car #1* | *Car #2* |
|---|---|---|
| Expiration date of present company 6/5/19—— | | |
| Bodily injury 50,000/100,000 | $40 | $40 |
| Property damage 50,000 | 30 | 30 |
| Medical payments or no-fault 50,000 | 20 | 20 |
| Uninsured motorist 50,000/100,000 | 8 | 8 |
| Collision less deductible of 100, 200, 500 | 50 | — |
| Comprehensive less deductible of 50, 100, 200, 500 | 32 | 32 |
| Towing, Rental reimbursement or other coverages | — | — |
| Subtotal | 180 | 130 |
| Total semiannual premium | $310 | |
| Total annual premium | $620 | |

coverage from the date indicated in lieu of the actual policy) before allowing the old policy to cancel out. Verify that the binder date corresponds to the expiration date of your old policy so that you don't pay for duplicate coverage or have a lapse in coverage.

## Car Insurance Comparison Chart

| *Prospective Company A Car #1—Car #2* | *Prospective Company B Car #1—Car #2* | *Prospective Company C Car #1—Car #2* |
|---|---|---|
| | | |
| ______ | ______ | ______ |

## How to Switch Insurance Companies for Maximum Premium Savings

Whenever the premium savings are substantial enough, you can switch immediately to a new company and avoid waiting for the next renewal or payment period, because any short-rata return (premium penalty) of your prepaid premium (15–20 percent less than what is prepaid and due you) will be more than offset by the present and future premium savings.

For example, if the new insurer's rate can save you $50 semiannually or $100 a year, it would definitely pay you to switch over immediately, even if you prepaid your present company $200 and would only get $160 of it returned due to the short-rata premium penalty ($200 prepaid premium − $40 or 20 percent short-rata penalty = $160 return of your prepaid premium). In this situation, your immediate gain would be $10 ($50 semiannual premium savings − $40 short rata penalty = $10 net gain), while the long-term savings would be $100 every year.

In most cases, the only requirement would be that your former insurance company would want its auto policy returned, along with a letter stating that you are now insured with the new company and wish your prepaid premium returned as soon as possible. Your new insurance representative should be more than happy to take care of the matter and, with his or her assistance, it shouldn't take longer than two weeks to have your refund check returned. See sample letters I and J.

## SAMPLE LETTER I

Requesting the refund of your prepaid premium from the former insurance company or from the former insurance broker.

6/10/81
John/Jane Policyholder
110 Washington Ave.
Anywhere, U.S.A.
Old Policy # 60-475-120-89

A.B.C. Insurance Company or
Your Former Insurance Broker
250 State St.
Anywhere, U.S.A.

Dear Insurance Company or Former Insurance Broker:

This is to inform you that as of 6/10/81 my auto insurance coverage will be handled by the X.Y.Z. Insurance Company under binder # or new policy #

In order that I may receive a prompt refund of my $200 prepaid premium, as well as for your convenience, I enclose your previous auto insurance policy.

I thank you for your full cooperation in this matter and for the timely refund of my prepaid premium.

Sincerely,
John/Jane Policyholder

## SAMPLE LETTER J

Requesting your state insurance department to assist you with the refund of your prepaid premium.

7/11/81

John/Jane Policyholder
110 Washington Ave.
Anywhere, U.S.A.
Old Policy # 60-475-120-89

State Insurance Department
Division of Consumer Affairs
100 Capitol St.
Anystate, U.S.A.

Dear Insurance Department:

I enclose a copy of my letter dated 6/10/81 which I sent to the A.B.C. Insurance Company or Former Insurance Broker requesting the refund of my prepaid premium.

After waiting for over a month, I still haven't

received my check and, therefore, I request your immediate assistance in lieu of my taking this to a small-claims court, my giving this to my attorney for additional action, or my taking this up with my congressman.

Please contact me as soon as possible so that this urgent matter can be settled promptly.

Again, I thank you for your timely assistance.

Sincerely,
John/Jane Policyholder

cc: A.B.C. Insurance Co. or
Former Insurance Broker

If the premium savings are not substantial enough to offset the short-rata prepaid premium penalty, you could simply wait to make the change at the next renewal or payment period.

If the new company's rate saves you only $30 semiannually or $60 a year, it would not pay you to make an immediate change since the short-rata prepaid premium penalty would be $10 more than the new premium savings ($200 prepaid premium × .20 short-rata penalty = $40 − $30 premium savings = $10 net loss). In this case, you should simply make the change at the next renewal or payment period and allow your former company to cancel you out for nonpayment of premium. You wouldn't be required to return the old policy or write an explanatory letter as in the previous case.

Whenever shopping around for a lower premium, use the Car Insurance Comparison Chart as a basis for comparing the rates of the various companies on your list of eligible insurers.

## Finding a Lower Rate with a Poor Driving Record

If your driving record is very poor (a total of two or more chargeable accidents or a total of two or more moving violations in a three-year period), or if you're an inexperienced driver with less than three years' driving experience, you might be able to find refuge with a group auto insurance plan if one is available through your employer or through a family member. At this time, there aren't too many group plans available, but I suspect there will be a lot of growth in the future in this particular area of auto insurance.

The chief advantage of these plans is that, like group hospitalization programs, they have no underwriting requirements, which means that everyone is accepted regardless of driving record. Therefore, these group auto plans offer those with unfortunate driving records an opportunity to leave the assigned risk plan and save 50 percent or more with the lower group rates. In view of such favorable rates, I strongly suggest that you seek out the availability of these plans either through your job or through an eligible family member.

Finally, if you're unable to insure through a group auto plan, you could try to locate an insurance representative who has been given "extended underwriting authority" from his or her insurance company. The extended underwriting authority allows the representative to accept at standard rates inexperienced drivers as well as those with poor operating records, who otherwise would be rejected and sent to the assigned risk plan.

The best way to find a representative with the extended underwriting authority is to call as many insurance companies and offices as possible, explain your circumstances, and express your desire to speak to any representative with such authority. This process may involve a few days' work and numerous phone calls, but, once located, the huge savings (50 percent +) will more than compensate you for the time spent.

# 6

# A Final Word

You, like all other drivers, deserve the lowest possible auto insurance premiums that are available not only for the present moment, but for the rest of your driving life. In order to ensure that your premiums will always remain at their lowest possible levels, I urge you to use this guide as a companion reference because when your driving circumstances change, so do the underwriting rules and rate classifications, which must be periodically monitored.

## Getting Help from Your State Insurance Department

Always remember that if you ever have a dispute with an insurance representative or, in particular, with an insurance company—either over a premium saving or over a refund matter—never hesitate to call or write your state insurance department, which was established to assist you with these problems. In fact, you'll find your department of insurance not only well equipped, but very supportive and consumer conscious when it works on your case. It is *you* who are in command and not the insurance company. Do not lose sight of that fact and you will never be abused by any insurance company or by any agent or broker.

Finally, don't ever return to making the same old mistakes. Don't become too complacent or forget to shop around occasionally for the lowest insurance rates. Any insurance rate structure or policy can adversely change overnight and with very little warning.

Keep your guard up and remember the principles outlined in this book and you'll have a smile on your face instead of a frown when it comes time to write out your car insurance check.

Good luck and happy savings!

## State Insurance Departments

Alabama Insurance
Department
Administrative Building
Montgomery, Alabama
36104
(205) 832-6140

Alaska Insurance
Department
State Office Building
Juneau, Alaska 99811
(907) 456-2515

Arizona Insurance
Department
1601 West Jefferson
Phoenix, Arizona 85007
(602) 271-4862

Arkansas Insurance
Department
12th & University
Avenue
Little Rock, Arkansas
72204
(501) 371-1325

California Insurance
Department
600 South
Commonwealth
Los Angeles, California
90005
(213) 620-2580

Colorado Insurance
Department
106 State Office Building
Denver, Colorado 80203
(303) 892-3201

Connecticut Insurance
Department
Room 425, State Office
Building
Hartford, Connecticut
06115
(203) 566-5275

Delaware Insurance
Department
21 The Green
Dover, Delaware 19901
(302) 678-4251

District of Columbia
Insurance Department
614 H Street N.W., Suite 512
Washington, D.C. 20001
(202) 629-4514

Florida Insurance Department
State Capitol
Tallahassee, Florida 32304
(904) 488-7056

Georgia Insurance Department
238 State Capitol
Atlanta, Georgia 30334
(404) 656-2056

Guam Insurance Department
P.O. Box 2796
Agana, Guam 96910

Hawaii Insurance Department
P.O. Box 3614
Honolulu, Hawaii 96811
(808) 548-7505

Idaho Insurance Department
206 State House
Boise, Idaho 83720
(208) 384-2250

Illinois Insurance Department
160 N. LaSalle Street, Room 1600
Chicago, Illinois 60601
(312) 793-2420

Indiana Insurance Department
509 State Office Building
Indianapolis, Indiana 46204
(317) 633-4892

Iowa Insurance Department
State Office Building
Des Moines, Iowa 50319
(515) 281-5705

Kansas Insurance Department
State Office Building
Topeka, Kansas 66612
(913) 296-3071

Kentucky Insurance Department
Capitol Plaza Tower
Frankfort, Kentucky 40601
(502) 564-3630

Louisiana Insurance Department
P.O. Box 44214, Capitol Station
Baton Rouge, Louisiana 70804
(504) 389-5671

Maryland Insurance Department
One South Calvert Bldg.
Baltimore, Maryland 21202
(301) 383-5690

Massachusetts Insurance Department
100 Cambridge Street
Boston, Massachusetts 02202
(617) 727-3357

Michigan Insurance Department
111 North Hosmer Street
Lansing, Michigan 48913
(517) 373-0220

Minnesota Insurance Department
Metro Square Building
St. Paul, Minnesota 55101
(612) 296-6907

Mississippi Insurance Department
P.O. Box 79
Jackson, Mississippi 39205
(601) 354-7711

Missouri Insurance Department
P.O. Box 690
Jefferson City, Missouri 65101
(314) 751-2451

Montana Insurance Department
Capitol Building
Helena, Montana 59601
(406) 449-2040

Nebraska Insurance Department
1335 L. Street
Lincoln, Nebraska 68508
(402) 471-2201, Ex. 20

Nevada Insurance Department
Nye Building
Carson City, Nevada 89710
(702) 885-4270

New Hampshire Insurance Department
169 Manchester
Concord, New Hampshire 03301
(603) 271-2261

New Jersey Insurance Department
201 East State Building
Trenton, New Jersey 08625
(609) 292-5363

New Mexico Insurance Department
P.O. Drawer 1269
Santa Fe, New Mexico 87501
(505) 827-2451

New York Insurance Department
Two World Trade Center
New York, New York 10047
(212) 488-4124

North Carolina Insurance Department
P.O. Box 26387
Raleigh, North Carolina 27611
(919) 829-7343

North Dakota Insurance Department
Capitol Building, Fifth Floor
Bismarck, North Dakota 58501
(701) 224-2244

Ohio Insurance Department
447 E. Broad Street
Columbus, Ohio 43215
(614) 466-3584

Oklahoma Insurance Department
408 Will Rogers Memorial Bldg.
Oklahoma City, Oklahoma 73105
(405) 521-4246

Oregon Insurance Department
158 12th Street, N.E.
Salem, Oregon 97310
(503) 378-4271

Pennsylvania Insurance Department
108 Finance Building
Harrisburg, Pennsylvania 17120
(717) 787-5173

Puerto Rico Insurance Department
P.O. Box 3508
San Juan, Puerto Rico 00904
(809) 722-0141

Rhode Island Insurance Department
100 North Main Street
Providence, Rhode Island 02903
(401) 277-2223

South Carolina Insurance Department
2711 Middleburg Drive
Columbia, South Carolina 29204
(803) 758-2185

South Dakota Insurance Department
Insurance Building
Pierre, South Dakota 57501
(605) 224-3563

Tennessee Insurance Department
114 State Office Building
Nashville, Tennessee 37219
(615) 741-2241

Texas Insurance Department
1110 San Jacinto Boulevard
Austin, Texas 78786
(512) 475-2273

Utah Insurance Department
275 E. Second South Street
Salt Lake City, Utah 84111
(801) 533-5611

Vermont Insurance Department
State Office Building
Montpelier, Vermont 05602
(802) 828-3301

Virginia Insurance Department
700 Blanton Building
Richmond, Virginia 23209
(804) 786-3741

Virgin Islands Insurance
Department
P.O. Box 450
Charlotte Amalie
St. Thomas, Virgin
Islands 00801
(809) 774-2991

Washington Insurance
Department
Insurance Building
Olympia, Washington
98504
(206) 753-7301

West Virginia Insurance
Department
1800 Washington Street, E.
Charleston, West
Virginia 25305
(304) 348-3386

Wisconsin Insurance
Department
123 West Washington
Madison, Wisconsin
53702
(608) 266-3583

Wyoming Insurance
Department
500 Randall Boulevard
Cheyenne, Wyoming
82001
(397) 777-7401

# Index


Accident-free rate, 89
Accidents
  collision coverage and, 42–45
  proving your innocence in, 44–45, 73–79
  rates policies for types of, 84–87
  *See also* At-fault accidents
Add-on discounts
  multi-car, 5–7, 40–41, 57–60
  nonprincipal operator, 14–16, 56–57, 59–61, 67–69
Adult/married rate. *See* Standard (1.00) rate; *and specific factors*
Age, rate classification and, 7–13
Annual mileage, rate classification and, 32–38
Assigned risk pool
  accident and violation record and, 23–25
  comprehensive and collision coverage and, 16–18
  inexperienced drivers and, 14
At-fault accidents
  avoiding penalties for, 79–81
  D.M.V. record and, 23–25
  premium surcharges for, 16–18
  youthful drivers and, 60–61

Car Insurance Comparison Chart, 94–95
Car pooling, 27–28
Collision coverage, 41–45, 47
  assigned risk pool and, 16–18
  explanation of, 41
  need for, 44–45
Commercial vehicles, 40
Comparison shopping for lowest rates, 91–95, 100–1
Comprehensive coverage, 41–42, 45–47
  assigned risk pool and, 16–18
  explanation of, 41–42

Deductible, for comprehensive and collision coverage, 42–44, 46–47
Department of Motor Vehicles (D.M.V.) record
  getting a copy of, 25
  period of, 23–25, 87–88
  rate classification and, 23–25
  *See also* Driving record
Discounts
  accident-free, 89
  for senior citizens, 12
  for single females aged 30–64, 11–12

for youthful drivers, 57–60
good driver, 89
limited usage, 25–29
low mileage, 32–38
multi-car, 5–7, 40–41, 57–60
Divorced marital status
premium reductions and refunds and, 19–22
rate classification and, 13
Driver training discount, 57–59
Driving record
poor, lower rate opportunities with, 100–1
*See also* Department of Motor Vehicles record; Maintaining a clean driving record

Extended underwriting authority, 101

Females
discount for 30–64 aged single, 11–12
rate classifications of, 10–13
Foreign countries, car insurance in, 52–53

Garage location of vehicle, 3–4, 38–40
Good driver discount, 89
Good student discount, 57–59
Group auto plans, 100–1

Income taxes, comprehensive and collision deductibles and, 46–47
Inexperienced drivers
lower rate opportunities for, 100–1
rate classification and, 13–18
*See also* Youthful drivers
Insurance agent, 2–3, 90
Insurance broker, 2–3, 90
Insurance companies, rate structure policies among, 82–89
Insurance representatives, 2–3
choosing the right, 89–90
with "extended underwriting authority," 101

Liability coverage, 47–55
*See also specific types of coverage*
Limits of liability, 47–51
states with minimum, 55
Location of vehicle garage, 3–4, 38–40
Low mileage discount, 32–38
premium reduction and refund for, 35–38
Lowest rates, shopping for, 91–95, 100–1

Maintaining a clean driving record, 71–81
  avoiding and contesting speeding tickets and other moving violations, 71–73
  avoiding premium surcharges and penalties and, 79–81
  proving your innocence in accidents and, 73–79
Males, rate classifications of, 7–10
Marital status
  rate classifications and, 7–13
  *See also* Divorced marital status; Newlywed couples
Medical payments coverage, 51
Mileage, annual
  rate classification and, 32–38
  *See also* Vehicle use
Motorcycles, mopeds, and motor scooters, 6
Moving violations
  avoiding and contesting, 71–73
  D.M.V. record and, 23–25
  premium surcharge for, 16–18
  rates policies for, 83–86
  youthful drivers and, 60–61
Multi-car discount, 5–7, 40–41
  youthful drivers and, 57–60

New (or newer) vehicle
  comprehensive and collision rates and model of, 45
  limited usage classification and, 27–28
  low mileage discount and, 34
  youthful driver and avoiding rating on, 67–69, 88–89
Newlywed couples
  rate classifications and, 12–13
  youthful drivers who are, 69
No-fault (personal injury protection) coverages, 51–52, 54
  states with, 54
Nonprincipal operator classification
  inexperienced drivers and, 14–16
  youthful drivers and, 56–57, 59–61, 67–69
Number of vehicles, rate classification and, 40–41

Operator license experience, rate classification and, 13–18

Parents, premium reductions and refunds for surcharged, 61–65
Personal injury protection (no-fault) coverages, 51–52, 54
Premium reductions and refunds
  limited usage and, 29–32
  low mileage discount and, 35–38
  parents and, 61–65
  separated or divorced spouses and, 19–22
Premium surcharge penalty, 16–18
  avoiding, 79–81
  driving record period and, 23–25, 87–88
  reductions and refunds for, 19–22
Prepaid premium
  requesting refund of, 97–99
  short-rata penalty, 96, 99
Principal operator, criteria of, 8
Public transportation, 27–28

Rate classifications, 1–55
  accident and violation record and, 23–25
  age, sex, and marital status and, 7–13
  annual mileage and, 32–38
  base premium rates and, 3–5
  collision and comprehensive coverage and, 41–47
  factors, 1–2
  limits of liability, uninsured motorist coverage, no-fault and medical payments coverage and, 47–55
  multi-car/vehicle add-on discount and, 5–7, 40–41, 57–60
  number of vehicles and, 40–41
  operator license experience and, 13–18
  standard (1.00), 3–5
  vehicle garage location and, 3–4, 38–40
  vehicle use and, 25–32
Rate structure policies, guide to fair, 82–89
Record, driving. *See* Driving record
Risk driver pool. *See* Assigned risk pool

Senior citizens
  discount for, 12
  rates policies for, 87
Separated couples. *See* Divorced marital status
Sex, rate classifications and, 7–13
Shopping for lowest rates
  guidelines for, 91–95
  poor driving record and, 100–1
Short-rata prepaid

Short-rata *(continued)*
premium penalty, 96, 99
Speeding tickets
avoiding and contesting, 71–73
*See also* Moving violations
Sports car, youthful driver and, 66–67
Spouse's policy add-on, inexperienced driver and, 15–16
Standard (1.00) rate classification, 3–5
State insurance departments, 102–9
listing of, 104–9
Surcharge penalty. *See* Premium surcharge penalty
Switching companies for maximum premium savings, 95–100

Umbrella personal liability policies, 53–54
Uninsured motorist (U.M.) coverage, 48–51

Vehicle add-on discount, 5–7, 40–41
youthful drivers and, 57–60
Vehicle garage location, 3–4, 38–40
Vehicle use
premium reductions and refunds and, 28–32
rate classifications and, 25–32
Violations. *See* Moving violations

Youthful drivers, 56–70
multi-car, driver training, and good student discounts, 57–59
new (or newer) vehicle coverage and, 67–69, 88–89
nonprincipal operator classification and, 56–57, 59–61
other valuable saving strategies for, 66–70
*See also* Inexperienced drivers; Parents